TOUCHING
THE HEART OF GOD

Embracing the Calendar of the Kingdom

PAUL WILBUR

FIRST EDITION

ISBN: 978-0-9965713-3-3

Library of Congress Control Number: 2015947687

Published by

CERTA BOOKS
partner publishing

P.O. Box 2839, Apopka, FL 32704

Printed in the United States of America

Table of Contents

Foreword

Most people experience Paul Wilbur as a musician—a very good and extremely anointed one at that. We pick up his CDs and play them over and again because of the way they usher us into God's presence. In *Touching the Heart of God: Embracing the Calendar of the Kingdom*, he who normally ushers in the presence of God with his guitar will usher us into God's presence with his pen—by presenting fresh insights into the Kingdom of God and God's heart for unity between Jewish and Gentile believers.

Those of us who travel with Paul occasionally get more than the musical CD version of the man and his ministry. Beyond "live-and-in-concert," we get to experience him stepping away from the guitar every now and then to stand up as a minister of the Word with his Bible in hand. In this capacity, Pastor Paul (or "Rabbi" Paul, if one prefers) likes to challenge us with a biblical point, much like he encourages people to experience Jesus through his music. Those of us privileged to get the non-musical "off-stage" version of Paul Wilbur encounter a light-hearted guy who is a lot of fun—but one who is also pointedly serious about his biblical study and teaching. We get Paul the theologian, and that is who you're going to get in this book.

Typically and appropriately, music ministers accompany evangelists and pastor-teachers to work with them in all kinds of settings—crusades, revivals, church services and the like. They work with a sense that the principal ministry moment belongs to "the man with the preaching-teaching message," and the worship leader makes ready that moment. Paul not only does this, but far more. Working side-by-side with him through his *Days of Elijah* conferences, I have had occasion to experience Paul stepping out from the role of "serving up the music" alone, to speaking directly and authoritatively to a variety of pastoral and theological issues. With the same mastery that he brings to his music, Paul picks up his Bible and gives voice to the Word of the Lord. He helps us take a look at neglected biblical underpinnings, beginning with an oft-misunderstood concept of the *Kingdom of God*.

He exposes modern readers to concepts of kings, kingdoms, citizenry, government, constitution, and the like. The need to pause and look at these is prompted by our social distance from this language—thus creating distance between ourselves and these essential biblical concepts. Given that believers are said to have entered the Kingdom of God (see John 3:3, 5), it is not beyond reason to expect that we should know something about the actual kingdom experience. The truth is most of us don't know, as we are far removed in space and time from the period or age when kings actually ruled. To aid us, by means of this book, Paul helps us to journey back in time and fills in some gaps of our understanding.

We live in a modern world wracked by social unrest and political intrigue. In this world, where leadership is in high demand but short supply, Paul Wilbur believes a fresh encounter with biblical Kingdom concepts isn't just a good idea, but a must!

Touching the Heart of God: Embracing the Calendar of the Kingdom exposes readers to the spiritual constitution of the Kingdom that undergirded ancient Israel's social and religious life. Paul brings into full view principles of the Kingdom that have direct bearing on Jesus of Nazareth—the One called *Yeshua*, Israel's Messiah. We learn in this wonderful book what it is to live in His domain and deal with experiences associated with walking alongside Him in this present age.

By reading this book and meditating upon its insights, you will be motivated even more to attend to the "Father's business" and His heart. With a cast of other messianic theologians who have endorsed Paul personally and weighed in on this book specifically, I give a hearty *thumbs-up* and wish you all God's best now as you carefully read through its pages.

Dr. Jeffrey Seif
University Distinguished Professor of Bible and Jewish Studies
Kings University-Houston.
Vice President/Project Manager, Tree of Life Bible

Introduction

As I travel around the world leading worship, I have the opportunity to connect with some amazing people. People of many languages, nations, cultures and religious backgrounds come together to honor the One True God—*the Great I AM*. In times of worship together, we have the privilege of *Touching the Heart of God* as He opens the very eyes of our hearts to know Him more. He invites us into His presence, to come experience Him and delight in Him, that we may know what is on His heart and join Him in what He is doing today!

Just as an earthly father takes joy in seeing his family grow in unity and strength as it moves forward in life, so our heavenly Father desires unity in those He calls family. From the time of Adam, through the calling and establishment of Israel, to the calling and establishment of the Church, God has been building a people—His family—to advance His Kingdom throughout the world. As Jews and Gentiles alike draw close in unity to Messiah Yeshua (Jesus) in worship, the Father smiles.

One of the great things about times of worship is that God seems to open the eyes of our understanding and brings about clarity. In His presence, wisdom and revelation flow like living waters, pride and strife seem to melt away, and there is fullness of joy.

For years now, God has been "connecting the dots" of my understanding about life in His Kingdom, and He has highlighted for me a critical element that has been greatly ignored over the centuries—the Calendar of God's Kingdom. Much has been written and preached to date about Kingdom theology, doctrine, government, and economics, but little has been said about the celebrations or the victories of our King, the Feasts of the Lord (Leviticus 23), and their continued significance for today's body of believers. So I am giving voice to my laptop keyboard (instead of my guitar) to highlight the incredible impact the Calendar of God's Kingdom can have on our lives today!

My intention in writing this book was not to be seen from the vantage point of a messianic believer who is wagging his finger in the air, scolding the Church saying, "You should be more like us over here." Rather, it is written from the place of a messianic believer, a member of the Kingdom of God, who loves the Church, as well as the messianic movement, and asks the question, "Shouldn't we all look more like *them*—the believers of the first century, Jewish and Gentile believers who loved God and one another?" What we see in the book of Acts and early church history is the Remnant, chosen from Israel, worshiping with the called out ones from the nations, celebrating the King of all Kings. This book is about recovering and restoring this knowledge and unity today. Jesus prayed His High Priestly Prayer in John 17 that we may *truly* be one. It is my observation that we don't experience this in the Kingdom today as we should, but God wants this to be so. It is *His heart*.

So how did the first century believers understand the Scriptures? What was important to them on a daily basis? How, and when, did they worship and celebrate? How does all of this apply to believers today—Jew and Gentile?

Yes, culture is important, and yes, our understanding can even change through time and events, but are there not eternal truths that are transcultural and *not* subject to change? After all, we were not called to be a sub-culture of any nation. Rather, we were called to be a counter-culture that leads the nations to the knowledge of the one true and living

God—the God of Abraham, Isaac, and Jacob!

I believe the Word of God, the Tanakh (also called the Old Testament) and the New Covenant (New Testament) to be one continuous revelation to one people of God. These people are made up of Jews and Gentiles, out of every tribe, tongue, and nation. They have been called, chosen, and loved by God since the foundation of the earth, destined to be one nation, holy and separate unto

After all, we were not called to be a sub-culture of any nation. Rather, we were called to be a counter-culture that leads the nations to the knowledge of the one true and living God.

God. *We* are those people! We are called to be different from all the other peoples of the earth. The way we dress, how we do business, how we speak and act, and even how we celebrate—are all manifestations of a chosen people united within the Kingdom of God. It is my belief that we need more of this in the Kingdom today.

The songs I write and sing are chiseled out of the rock of the Word of God because they carry a promise—the promise that those words will not return void, but they will accomplish the task for which they have been sent out from heaven. Millions have sung these songs and allowed King Jesus' message to bless their hearts and minds. I may not hold doctorates in theology, archeology, Hebrew, or Greek, but I do know something about *Touching the Heart of God*. It is my prayer that Messiah Yeshua will expand our understanding of our common Judeo-Christian roots and propel us forward in power and unity, while serving the King and His Kingdom.

I realize that we all come to the concepts in this book from differing backgrounds and vantage points. I pray that you will walk patiently with me, as I present the case for the Father's heart and the Calendar of God's Kingdom. Unity can only spring from humility. So humbly, I ask you to prayerfully read and consider what is written in the following pages.

When Jesus (*Yeshua* in the Hebrew, which I will use

interchangeably throughout this work, without any further explanation) walked among us on this earth (in the days of His flesh), He often taught

Unity can only spring from humility.

by use of parables—stories that have a deeper and often, hidden meaning. Here's my version of a parable I am offering to make a point, which I hope is not so hidden. It will help illustrate the heart of what I intend to accomplish with the writing of this book.

A Modern Day Parable

Many years ago in a kingdom far, far away, there lived a great man with a large family. He was so kind and loving that he decided to expand his family, through adoption, to anyone who cared to join. He carefully crafted the invitation and publicly posted it for all to see. He sent messengers to travel around the world inviting foreigners and strangers to join his family and enjoy the blessings of his house. This father's love was so great that one day he sent his own son out to demonstrate his love and invite the world to come in.

Soon his family began to grow by leaps and bounds, sometimes by thousands a day. They came from far and near and from every kind of background. Before long, the good, the bad, and the outcast were sitting at his table, enjoying the blessings of this great man, who had now become their father. Those first adoptions went very well. The new heirs were eager to join in the celebrations of their father. They found themselves looking forward to the weekly day of rest, when they closed their shops and left their work behind. They refreshed themselves, shared time with their brothers and sisters, as well as their father. Many were added to the family during those days, as word began to spread about the generosity of this household. Not only was their daily bread provided, but there was also healing and forgiveness for all, no matter who they had been before their adoption or from where they had come. What an amazing father this man was! His generosity was even imitated by his own children. If someone in the family had a need, the other children sold their own possessions in order that no one would go without.

As the family grew, it added even more people from many different countries, cultures, and languages, just as the father had envisioned. The family included the lame, the blind, the sick, the wealthy, the poor, the humble, and the great. They had very little in common, except for their love for the father and his son, who had personally extended the father's invitation to them to come be a part of his father's family.

But these new family members, brought in by adoption, had no understanding of the family's history, ways, and traditions. Although they were glad to be a part of this new family, they began to challenge the "necessity" of being present at all the family celebrations. And so, one by one, little by little, they stopped coming to the gatherings. Eventually, they ceased to even respond to the invitations. As their own families grew across the nations, some ceased to teach their own children about the ways of their father. They began to adopt the customs and celebrations of the nations in which they lived. Some of them went to school and studied with learned men who taught them it was wrong, maybe even dishonoring to the family, to celebrate the traditional feasts and victories of the father. "All of that is under the old ways of the household," they said. "We have been set free from the heaviness and bondage of those early days of obedience." The children had forgotten the words of their older brother who said to his Father on Mount Sinai, "teach me *your* ways so I may know you and continue to find *favor* with you" (Ex. 33:13).

Some of the children became confused by all of this. They still wanted to go to the father's house during the appointed times of celebration, as had been their tradition. They were ridiculed for this and called names by their "enlightened" brothers and sisters. *Legalist* or *heretics* were some of the names flung at them, as they gathered to celebrate the family history. Some were also rejected by members of their own family for even considering being a part of such things! Before long, it was almost impossible to recognize some of the children as having been adopted by that generous man of so many years ago. Their ways had now become so removed from that of their father's house. The family became splintered, fractured, and dysfunctional. They couldn't even agree to meet with one another anymore. What became of this family? Their older, much wiser brother, the father's son, who had come to seek them out on behalf of the father, prayed for them many years ago and continues to intercede for them with his father even today. [His prayer: "…that all of them may be one, Father, just as you are in me and I am in you. May they also be in *us* so that the world may believe that you have sent me" (John 17:21; emphasis added).]

My heart, as you read this book, is that the Father will bring us all to a greater place of understanding and unity, for this is the Father's heart.

PART 1

CHAPTER 1

It's His Kingdom

The Kingdom of God

In Matthew 6:33, we read these familiar words: "But seek first His Kingdom and His righteousness, and all these things will be given to you as well." What do you think when you hear the word *Kingdom*? Does it speak to you about a place, or perhaps a religion; maybe it communicates a concept or a philosophy? Well, the Kingdom of God is none of these things. To understand what the Kingdom of God is—a Kingdom "not of this world"—let's first look at what it is *not*.

The Kingdom is Not a Democracy

The Kingdom is NOT a democracy or a republic. It is not *of the people, by the people,* nor *for the people.* There are no democratically elected agents of the Kingdom who can be voted in or out depending on how we feel about them, or based on the job they are doing. The Kingdom is not the Church, and the Church did not create it. There are no angels who vacate their positions to bump up to higher posts, leaving an open harp to be claimed by the most popular angel of the week.

Then what is the Kingdom of God?

The Kingdom of God is a Theocracy (God-ruled)

The Kingdom of God is the King's domain, where His word and law reign, without challenge or contestation. He doesn't change. He's the same yesterday, today, and forever. The same goes for His throne, His Word, and His ways!

In the book of Revelation, chapter four, heaven is opened to us and we get a glimpse of the King who sits on the throne. He has the appearance of jasper and ruby. There is a rainbow, like an emerald encompassing the throne, and there are twenty-four elders seated on thrones surrounding His. It is presented as an awesome sight of brightness and majesty, with a sea of crystal glass and strange creatures covered with eyes on every side of their bodies. There are flashes of lightning and crashes of thunder. The creatures about the throne are speaking day and night, and they never stop declaring:

"Holy, holy, holy, is the Lord God Almighty, who was, and is, and is to come" (Rev. 4:8).

"Who was" perhaps represents the revelation to Simon Peter, who recognized Jesus of Nazareth as the true Messiah of Israel, when he declared in Matthew 16:16, "You are the Messiah, the Son of the Living God." "Who is" may be the revelation to Paul, who boldly preached Yeshua in the synagogues of the known world of his day. And "who is to come" may very well be the revelation to John, while marooned on the Isle of Patmos for his faith, and who had a great vision of the return of the Lord in Revelation 19:11-16. We could all use a fresh revelation of the *One who was, who is, and who is to come*! This is no wimpy "religious figure" dressed in a gown and sandals with a bluebird sitting upon his shoulder. This is the King of ALL Kings, the Lion of the Tribe of Judah, the Warrior King, who comes with fury to enforce the wrath of God Almighty! That's the King we worship!

If someone thinks the rules aren't quite fair in God's Kingdom, which is His domain, attaining a majority vote will not cause this King to alter His rules. He will not remove the Ten Commandments from His halls of justice in order to please man's carnal sensitivities. Man did not script the laws of the constitution of the Kingdom, nor will man be given the opportunity to amend them.

The Kingdom of God Has Laws of Finance and Blessing

Earthly kingdom treasuries are filled through the collection of taxes, the inheritances of succession, and the amassing of the spoils of war. The Kingdom of God is different. It is not sustained, nor is it maintained by the benevolent giving and offerings of its citizens. Its financial stability, and ongoing support, does not rest on the ability of its citizens to provide for it. As a matter of fact, it is actually the King of the Kingdom who provides for His own citizens! The King not only owns the Kingdom, but He owns the universe, the earth and all its fullness, and the cattle on a thousand hillsides. All silver and gold is His. Even the lives of the subjects (that is, you and me) belong to Him. King Yeshua owns all things, has created all things, and needs nothing whatsoever! He sustains all things by the power of His Word.

The financial system of the world is driven by buying and selling. You put your "shekels" on the counter, and you receive goods and services you can afford. "You get what you pay for" is how we say it.

If a president takes money from the treasury and gives it to someone he is pleased with, we call it theft. In fact, we would put such a president in jail. Why? Because he took money that didn't belong to him. However, when a king reaches into the treasury and blesses someone with land, houses, cars, and property, it is called *favor*! Why? Because in a kingdom, all the stuff belongs to the king— every penny, all the land, all the fields, all the crops, all the

With the favor of the king comes freedom from fear and lack.

herds and flocks, and yes, even the people. The king owns everything, everywhere, all the time. All the stuff is his to distribute at his good pleasure, whenever and to whomever he pleases. With the favor of the king comes freedom from fear and lack.

So, the Kingdom of God has a very different system for its

citizens to operate in—it is called *sowing and reaping*. In the Kingdom of God, we are given the privilege, and opportunity, to give to the King and His purposes on this earth. He provides the means from which we give our tithes and offerings, as we demonstrate our trust in God's provision. Through this giving, we invite the King to get involved in our personal finances, in order for us to be blessed through the spiritual principle of sowing and reaping. (Read Malachi 3, Mark 4, and Luke 8 to get greater clarity on this principle.)

The Kingdom of God has a Government

The Kingdom of God is orderly. It is governed by a body of laws and regulations, written by the King and enforced by Him and His agents. Just like in other kingdoms, these agents are given authority by the King and only answer to Him for their actions. There is a constitution with a "bill of rights," giving the citizens of the Kingdom certain privileges within the borders of the King's rule. And although, some may only view God's laws as limiting and restrictive, these laws actually provide authority, protection, and bring freedom to the citizens of the Kingdom.

Think of it this way: What if it was announced that starting tomorrow at 5:00 a.m. all rules and laws for driving on the major interstate near your house would be permanently suspended? Moreover, all policemen will be forbidden to patrol or ticket anyone driving on that road. How many would actually go anywhere near that highway again? Not this guy! Statutes, laws, and regulations are put in place for our personal safety and the common good—not merely to be legalistic.

Unfortunately, it seems to me, living in the Western Hemisphere, we have for centuries been inundated by a philosophy known as *antinomianism,* or against the establishment of moral law. This has turned our thinking against such foundations as the Torah, law, and absolute truth. Instead, we are asked to swallow some syrupy, sweet stuff hailed as grace, which is elevated over the very building blocks of our faith. We've all heard it many times: Old Covenant = Law = bad; New Covenant = grace = good. Well, which of the Ten Commandments are we willing to throw out? This is perhaps an oversimplification, but I see it as a problem nonetheless.

CHAPTER 2

The King

The Lineage of a King

The most important figure in any kingdom is, of course, the king. His right to rule is not through a democratic vote, but rather by right of birth and royal bloodline. In ancient times, the right of succession was written down and kept in vaults and treasuries. This was done in order to verify and validate the family name, protecting the throne from pretenders. Where did these bloodlines begin? Who were the first kings and from where did these kingdoms come? If we are speaking of the kingdoms of this world, then the answer is easy. Some time ago, our ancestors played *King of the Hill*. The one who remained standing at the end of the game was declared to be the winner and became king. He won the right to make the rules and the decisions, which everyone else had to follow. If another person came along and challenged that king and won, the new victor could run the show any way he saw fit. These kingdoms ascended, or fell from power, by virtue of the might of their armies and alliances. Often, the wealth of the kingdom became the determining factor for victory or defeat, as it was quite common to purchase a "gun-for-hire" to help out when the battle was too big to win through the kingdom's strength alone.

This is not so with the Kingdom of God. Jehovah or Yahweh (an educated guess at the name of the King, based on the four Hebrew letters: yod, hey, vav, hey) chose the man, Abram from Ur of the Chaldees. Although this man was the son of an idol maker and a moon worshiper, Abram was chosen to be *the man* whose bloodline would start the ball rolling. Later his name was changed to Abraham, meaning *the father of many nations*. Often, when kings chose people for a kingdom purpose, the names of those individuals were changed to fit the calling they had received. When we follow the bloodline of Abraham, we come to his son, Isaac (not Ishmael, as the Muslims teach); then Isaac's son, Jacob (who God renamed Israel); and then through Jacob's twelve sons (including Judah, where we get the name *Jew*). From the tribe of Judah, we trace the royal bloodline to the Messiah Himself. You may have asked at some time, why do we need to go through the laborious recitations of all the "begats" in the book of Numbers, or the long dissertation of the lineage of Yeshua in the Gospels? Well, for the simple reason that kingship is not open to chance or interpretation. Either you are in the royal line for succession to the throne or you are not. The case for the bloodline of Yeshua is clearly and accurately delineated, generation by generation, so that all may see that He has a rightful claim as the heir to the royal throne of His "father" King David of Jerusalem. Once this has been established, there is no room for debate or discussion—the case is closed.

Let me add a side note (and I will be brief here, as my good friend Michael L. Brown, Ph. D., author of the five-volume series: *Answering Jewish Objections to Jesus* and President of FIRE School of Ministry, considers this to be highly speculative). To whom was Yeshua really speaking in Matthew 23:39 when He said, "You will not see me any more until *you* say, 'Baruch haba b'shem Adonai'" (blessed is he who comes in the name of the Lord)? Many have thought it to be to the nation of Israel or all the Jewish people. Others have said, no, he was only speaking to Jerusalem. But we get insight into exactly whom Jesus was speaking of when He said, "I wanted to gather your children together as a hen gathers her chicks, but you were not willing" (*v.* 37). *Who* was not willing? Who were the hens of Jesus' day? Who were those carefully guarding the "chicken coop?" And who were those that flew in the face of any intruder who might steal *their* chicks? Was it not the Pharisees, Sadducees, and the Sanhedrin? They were the guardians of the Law, the words of the Torah, and the interpreters of the voice of Jehovah to the people of ancient Israel. And they, like the nation of Israel, had disappeared from the face of the earth for more than 1,900 years. I say *had* because as of late 2004, they are back again as a ruling eldership for the religious Jews of Israel! Indeed, the hens have returned to watch over the chicks, and will someday fulfill the words of Jesus, as they declare Him King of the Jews—"Baruch haba b'shem Adonai!"

Hallelujah, what a day that will be! The graves will open, and the mountain of the Lord will be split in two. We'll hear the shofar of God, the shout of the Angel of the Lord, and those who fell asleep in Messiah Jesus will rise first. Those of us who are still alive will be caught up together with them to meet the Lord at His coming, and forever we shall be with Him (1 Thess. 4:16-18). SELAH (meditate) on that for a little while, why don't you! It took nearly two millennia to resurrect the nation of Israel, get Jerusalem back into Jewish hands, and reassemble the Sanhedrin in order to make that prophetic declaration, but time is not a problem for the King of the Kingdom—the Lord of ALL creation!

The Authority of a King

What makes a king unique, if not the power of his words? When a president speaks, we analyze, criticize, armchair quarterback, and decide whether or not we like what he said and how he said it. Then, we voice how we would have done it differently if we were in his shoes. In fact, we judge him for his actions and decide whether or not to keep him in office. Don't try that with a king, especially the King of Kings—He is not voted in or out.

When a king speaks, it is law. And his law cannot be changed. This is why a wise king doesn't speak very much and never speaks frivolous words, which he does not intend to back up. Some would say that kings don't have a good sense of humor. I would say that wise kings have a great sense of the weightiness of each word they speak. They know the power they wield with each word spoken. Do you want to be blessed? Get the king to speak to you! When he does, he will do what he says. The king's reputation depends on his faithfulness to do what he declared. His very character is defined by the quality of his words. The word of a righteous king is not only law for his subjects, but it is a covenant that binds and defines the king, as well.

The king's mouth holds the power to bless, curse, forgive, or to end a life. When a king spoke, his word was final and indisputable. His words were not to be challenged or questioned. They were to be obeyed explicitly. His words carried absolute authority, even if his judgment was questionable. Questioning the veracity of the king's word would introduce instability into a system, which would keep it from enduring. How else could Pharaoh get away with ordering the death of the male Hebrew babies in Exodus 1:16? Even the word of an evil king is followed to the letter of his command.

Remember the law that Haman convinced King Xerxes to make concerning the death of all the Jews? Queen Esther, his wife, couldn't get the law changed even after Haman was hanged on his own gallows. A new law had to be issued declaring the Jews could arm and defend themselves when the time came (See Esther 8:8).

In the book of Daniel, we are told that once King Nebuchadnezzar realized his law regarding worshipping the gold image, which he had created, meant the certain death of the three Hebrews in the fiery furnace (Shadrach, Meshach, and Abednego), he hated his own law. Nebuchadnezzar was later deceived into creating a law against the prayers of his friend, Daniel. He couldn't sleep worrying about the fate of Daniel in the lion's den that night. But even the king himself, the most powerful man in the kingdom, could not reverse the law once he had spoken the words. His word was the law, and it had to be fulfilled to the letter once it was declared. If he wished, he could make a new law in order to balance the first, but the first was never changed, nullified, or withdrawn. In these stories, we find out that God brought about the victorious protection for these men, who were at the mercy of the king's orders. The King of ALL Kings moved on their behalf.

Citizens of a Kingdom

Another important element of a kingdom is the people. People are known by another name in a kingdom. They are called *citizens*— not members of an organization with the right to vote at a meeting, but citizens with certain rights, privileges, and restrictions, as prescribed by the king. It may sound a bit radical, I admit, to state that the people of a kingdom actually belong to the king, but that *is* exactly how it goes. This may sound like a bad deal, until you consider the reputation of the king and his kingdom. This is exactly why you should carefully consider which king and kingdom you serve. I think Bob Dylan may have said it best with the words of his popular song "Gotta Serve Somebody"—*Now it might be the devil, or it might be the Lord, but you're gonna have to serve somebody!*

Let me remind you that there are only two choices when it comes to "kingdom shopping." There is the kingdom of darkness, where Satan (formerly Lucifer, while a part of the Kingdom of God) rules with demonic spirits to enforce his leadership. He rules with fear, rage, disease, torment, poverty, and the like. He makes certain that his citizens keep well within the boundaries of his domain.

Then there is the Kingdom of God. The major differences here are pretty simple. Jehovah is the Father of Light. He is the embodiment of love itself, and there is no shadow of turning with Him. He is a guardian of the weak, a protector of the orphan and widow. He made all things, and He sustains *all* things with His powerful word. He is good all the time, righteous, merciful, kind, long-suffering, and has a perfect track record when it comes to proving all that I have just stated. Righteousness, peace and joy are the virtues esteemed and dispensed from the throne of this King.

Now, which king and kingdom did you say you wanted to serve? I'll give you a few seconds more to make up your mind…Good choice!

Citizens of the Kingdom of God

So who are the people or citizens of the Kingdom of God? They are the ones who have believed the words of the King of Kings and, therefore, have entered into His Kingdom. Second Corinthians 5:17 (ISV) says it this way, "Therefore if any [man] is in the Messiah, he is a new creation…" But just for fun, try reading it in this paraphrased version: Therefore, if any man is in the Kingdom, he is a new citizen. All the old ways of living, and being, have changed, and because of the King, all things have been made new.

You have been delivered out of the kingdom of this world, the kingdom of darkness, and translated into the Kingdom of the Son—Jesus Christ. In His Kingdom, with King Jesus, we have redemption, even the forgiveness of sin. All aspects, which were ours in the other kingdom—death, slavery to sin, and debts, have been changed and made new. You have been born again into a new life!

This sounds really, really good, you say, *but doesn't this downplay the importance of the role of the King?* Not at all! You see, you cannot enter this new Kingdom without going through the entrance or gate. Yeshua said He was the door, or the gateway, for the sheep (John 10:7). He said, "I am the way, the truth and the life. No one comes to the Father [into His Kingdom] except through me" (John 14:6). If you want to get into the Kingdom of God, you must enter through the narrow gate (Matt. 7:13). There simply is no other way to get in.

Some may try to sell you a cheap ticket into this Kingdom through meditation, good works, prayers, idols, and offerings. Don't be deceived! This King only has *one* Kingdom with *one* door, and there is no other way given to men—under heaven—by which we could enter. This door is also known by the names: Savior, Anointed One, Yeshua HaMashiach, Jesus the Messiah, and King of the Jews. Call on His name, the door will open for you, and you will enter the Kingdom of God!

Imagine a Kingdom where brothers don't take legal action against one another simply because the law says not to treat your brother like that. What about a Kingdom where the divorce rate is so low among believers that it becomes a powerful testimony of the love of God, which has really been shed abroad in our hearts? What about a

Kingdom where heart disease and cancer are so rare that many doctors have to specialize in other disciplines?

Additionally, when you are a citizen of the Kingdom of God, when you enter the Kingdom, you receive a gift from the King. This gift is to be used for your good and the good of others. God told Abraham that He would bless him so that Abraham could bless the world. In Deuteronomy 8:18, the King said He provides the ability to produce wealth. Through those riches, He establishes His covenant (and Kingdom) on all the earth. The house you live in, the car you drive, your 401(k)—that's right—it's all on loan from the King. And, how we manage these resources will determine how much more He can trust us to oversee in this life and the life to come.

Here's one more little piece of good news: Your personal welfare and well-being is now the direct responsibility of the King you serve. How the people live is a direct reflection of their King, His glory and His reputation. This is why King Yeshua is pleased to give His citizens "all things to enjoy" (1 Tim. 6:17). These articles are all listed in the constitution of the Kingdom—the Bible. It is up to you, the citizen, to locate these blessings and activate them, by believing and acting on the Word of the King. This is what some of the citizens have come to know as *faith*.

CHAPTER 3

Getting in Step with the King's Rule

A King's Domain

Another important element of a kingdom is the territory ruled by the king—his *domain*. It is the place where his authority is exercised and enforced. (By the way, did you know that the word *kingdom* or *king-dom* is shorthand for *the king's domain*?) It is not a partnership, club, religion, nor a joint venture. It is a system of government, which is enforced with power and authority.

How does a king enforce the laws of his territory? By the power of his word. One demonstration of the power of God's spoken word is creation. We read in Scripture that God spoke, and all things seen and unseen were created. Today, scientists believe they have finally discovered the essential building blocks of the universe. Through the power of modern science, microscopes have peered inside the nucleus of an atom to view the matter, which is the foundation of all things. Do you know what they now believe is the glue holding all things together? Sound waves! And why not? In the beginning, God said, "Let there be..." and it came into being. It makes perfect sense that the sound of the King's voice, or sound waves, is the material from which all things have their being. The Scriptures also say that He sustains all things with His powerful word. The life you live, the goodness you experience, even the air you are breathing right now is a gift from Him to you. Enjoy!

He also rules His Kingdom through His mighty army. There is no military service or draft board in His kingdom. The citizens don't need to die to preserve His Kingdom. The King's Son, Jesus, already fought and died. Yet, He rose again to protect the citizens, and to establish the rule of the Kingdom over death and Hell itself. Can you imagine any other kingdom where the king sends out his own son to fight for the lives of the people? Outrageous! In every other kingdom, the people exist to serve the king. In *this* kingdom—the Kingdom of God—the King lives to love and protect His citizens. Amazing!

> In every other kingdom, the people exist to serve the king. In *this* kingdom—the Kingdom of God—the King lives to love and protect His citizens.

So who makes up this mighty army? Who are they that do the King's bidding and keep the people safe? The angels of the Most High God. They live to follow the King's commands, and fight on behalf of the King and His people. The King is the head of all principalities and powers (Col. 2:10). The angel armies are made up of incredible creatures, created by the King for such a purpose. When men have seen them, they are described as large beings wearing garments that shine like the sun. Some have been seen wielding massive flashing swords of light and fire. They are so magnificent in their appearance that men are tempted to worship them, but the Bible warns us not to do that. We are to serve and worship the King alone, the Creator of these beings. In fact, angels were also created to serve us, as we serve the King! He gave His angels charge over us so that we will not even strike our foot against a stone, lest we are harmed or taken out. (See Psalm 91)

Where is the King's domain? The Bible says the earth is the Lord's and everything in it. It also declares that the heavens, the seas, and all that is in them and under them belong to Him. In Matthew, Jesus declares that the Kingdom is at hand, or very near, and in Luke 17:21, He states, "The Kingdom is within."

His Beloved Israel

The King particularly loves a little strip of land, which borders the eastern shore of the Mediterranean Sea. He has a favorite city located approximately sixty miles from the coast in that same country. Yes, Israel and Jerusalem hold a special place in the King's heart like no other. This was the land promised to Abram when he was called to serve God. The covenant was reaffirmed with Abraham and Isaac on the mountain. The Promised Land is where King David, once a shepherd boy, ruled. Here David's son, King Solomon displayed a glory and wisdom no one before him, or since, has equaled. And this is the place Yeshua chose to pour out His covenant of blood, securing the Kingdom for all time and for all who would call on His Name.

When we understand the Father's love for Israel, we can see how anti-Semitism is an abomination to the Lord. All people, especially Christians, should remain compassionate toward the Jewish people, as they are going through horrific tribulation today. In fact, hatred toward Jews and all Christian people is increasing at an alarming rate.

Of His Government There Shall be No End

Having stated the case for God's Kingdom, as opposed to a mere religion, let me make one more point before moving on. This Kingdom can be summed up in terms of a *government*.

In the ninth chapter of the Book of Isaiah, the prophet speaks of a child who will sit on the throne of His father David. He goes on to call this child by names ascribed only to the Great King, and then states that the increase of His government will never end.

Make no mistake about it—this is exactly why the power brokers of His day feared what Jesus would do as a ruler and king. Herod knew of these prophecies and ordered the destruction of innocent children. The trial of Yeshua was a titan-sized clash of governments and kingdoms, not religions. During His "interview" with Pilate, in the eighteenth chapter of the gospel of John, Jesus acknowledged that He was born to be a King and that His Kingdom was not of this world. Before He was crucified, the Roman soldiers mocked him, dressing him like a pauper king. As a human pawn, He was moved about on a game board etched into the pavement stones of the Roman guardhouse. He was beaten with rods and whips. He was mocked with robes of royalty and a thorny crown, as the game played its way out to the ultimate cruel death on a Roman cross. Here the condemned died a slow and torturous death. Sometimes taking days, as the crucified slowly suffocated from their own bodily fluids. When Messiah was finally hung on that rugged cross, the sign placed above His head declared: "Yeshua of Nazareth, King of the Jews." The kingdoms of the Syrians, Greeks, Romans, Persians, and Meads have all come and gone, but the Kingdom of God and His Messiah remain forever.

The gospel, or good news, about God's Kingdom is its government—of this government there shall be no end! He rules all things, at all times and in all places. He is Master and Commander, Aleph and the Tav, Alpha and Omega (for those who prefer Greek over Hebrew), Beginning and End, and Baruch shem k'vod malchuto l'olam vaed. Blessed is His Name, whose glorious Kingdom is forever and ever, amen!

CHAPTER 4

God's Heart—
We Should Be One

The Kingdom Man and the One New Man

You know that God makes us a new creation upon salvation (2 Cor. 5:17). But did you know that Scripture addresses another intriguing principle about being made new—that of the One New Man—where Jews and Gentiles alike become one? Your understanding of this will color your view of the Kingdom. Your worship will be greatly affected as you embrace God's heart in this matter.

Let's take a look at how we were two...

Until the time of Christ, Gentiles were foreigners who were not included in the promises God made to Israel. Therefore, they were without hope and far removed from God and the Kingdom. Gentiles were the "uncircumcised" and called "unclean" by the Jews, and lived as a separate people.

But now, through the blood of Jesus shed on the cross, Jews and Gentiles have become one—One New Man. Both groups have been reconciled to God through Jesus' death and resurrection. All barriers between the two have been destroyed. Both groups now have access to the Father, and there should be peace among the two. It is the Father's heart that we come to this revelation and walk together in humility and in unity—Jew and Gentile—One New Man.

It is clear from the Scripture in Galatians 3:28, that *in the Spirit* "there is neither Jew nor Gentile, neither slave nor free, nor is there male and female, for you are all one in Christ Jesus." However, it is also clear in Scripture that for the sake of calling, identity, and just plain common sense, there are some real and important differences with all the aforementioned. There exists today, as in the time when Paul wrote to the Galatians, Jews and Gentiles, males and females, and it is good for us to know and discern the differences.

I believe the biggest mistake we could make when trying to define this Kingdom man is to try to somehow structure him into a universally recognizable person. One of the glorious aspects of this Kingdom is *unity with diversity*. I do not believe it is the King's intent that we all look, sound, or worship in the same manner and style. Rather, it is like the example of marriage, where there is unity and harmony, yet there are also differences, which are both apparent and not so apparent. There are also some obvious differences among people—between male and female, among the races, in size, strength, and other ways. But there are important differences that are not so obvious. These require more time to discern, such as temperaments, likes, hopes, dreams, emotions, and needs.

The manner in which we all do things will differ. In fact, we find distinguishable aspects even in the corporate worship styles of believers. There are certain outward differences, and I will limit my comments to that, without historical or emotional qualifiers. Naturally, there is an inclination to do things the way we were raised, or in the manner in which we have grown accustomed. Mature believers, however, should seek to understand and appreciate the differences that actually make us strong.

Where the One New Man Concept was Born

There are three passages of Scripture that I will highlight to get at the heart of this One New Man concept—Ephesians 2, John 17, and Psalm 133. First let's take a look at Ephesians 2. It is important to remember that the apostle Paul is writing to new Gentile believers at Ephesus. He wanted to encourage them in their faith, as well as in their new position as joint-heirs and fellow citizens with Jewish believers in the Kingdom of God.

> *Therefore, remember that formerly you who are Gentiles by birth and called "uncircumcised" by those who call themselves "the circumcision"… remember that at that time you were separate from Messiah, excluded from citizenship in Israel, and foreigners to the covenants of the promise, without hope and without God in the world. But now, in Christ Jesus, you who once were far away have been brought near through the blood of Christ.*
>
> *For he himself is our peace [Sar Shalom], who has made the two one and has destroyed the barrier, the dividing wall of hostility…His purpose was to create in himself ONE NEW MAN out of the two thus making peace, and in this one body to reconcile both of them to God through the cross…He came and preached peace to you who were far away [the Gentiles] and peace to those who were near [the Jews]. For through him we both have access to the Father by one Spirit.*
>
> *Consequently, you are no longer foreigners and strangers, but fellow citizens with God's people [the Jews] and also members of his household [the Kingdom]…*
>
> *And in him [Jesus the Messiah] you too are being built together to become a dwelling in which God lives by his Spirit.*
>
> —Ephesians 2:11-19, 22 (Emphasis added)

I like the New Living Translation version of verse fifteen where this is more fully described:

"By his death he ended the whole system of Jewish law that excluded the Gentiles. His purpose was to make peace between Jews and Gentiles by creating in himself one new person from the two groups" (Eph. 2:15).

As Yeshua said on the Mount of Beatitudes, He didn't come to destroy the law or the prophets, but to fulfill them by taking away the barriers, which had kept the nations from salvation and from entering the Kingdom with Israel.

So it goes without saying, Jesus gave His life to bridge the abyss between heaven and earth, and to make a covenant with us that would destroy the wages of sin, hell, death, and the grave. But He also destroyed the middle wall of partition between Jews and Gentiles. He made peace between us in that same act of obedient sacrifice. In fact, it is this unity that comes from faith in Him. This is one of the assurances to the world that Jesus really is Messiah (John 17:21)! I rejoice when, in our world today, there is reconciliation between the races, sexes, and societies. Yet, there is no greater earthly reconciliation than that of Jews and Gentiles in Christ.

During the first century, when most followers of Yeshua were Jewish by birth and Jewish in their expression of worship, the new Gentile converts to the New Covenant, simply joined a service already in progress. They worshiped with the rest of the Jewish believers in the traditional Jewish ways. They met together and traveled from house to house, breaking bread, singing, praying, and worshiping. What did their worship sound like? What kind of songs did they sing? Did they use any of the liturgical material from the Temple?

Today, we have a very different dynamic, which not only needs to be recognized but adjusted. We must make room for a fuller expression of what the Spirit of God is doing on the earth today. What do I mean by that? After 1,800 or so years of Gentile Christianity in the nations without a viable or numerable Jewish presence, we find ourselves in a time when many Jews are receiving the Messiah. They are seeking to worship in a way that reflects their lives, experiences, and authentic biblical history. This should be cause for great celebration in the Church, as acceptance of His grace by the Jews, according to the apostle Paul, means "*life from the dead*" (Rom. 11:15).

Unfortunately, in many churches, One New Man means very little to the new Jewish believer in Jesus. Can you see how difficult this would be for a Jew raised in a synagogue or temple, or even a non-religious home? How difficult would it be for him or her to walk into a church service and feel *at home*? Imagine yourself as a new Jewish believer, raised in a nominally religious home. You went to temple on Passover and Yom Kippur, and you completed the minimal religious studies as a child. Now come with me to a church service, where you stand to sing psalms and hymns you have never heard before and kneel at an altar in front of a life-sized, half-naked Jew nailed to a Roman cross. Next the minister approaches with a silver chalice, places a wafer stamped with a cross in your mouth and declares, "The body of Christ." You then hear a sermon about peace in the world, critical about Israel, and all the while you are thinking: *What in the world have I done? Will someone please tell me, is this the Jewish Messiah I received last week?*

Now, in order to be fair, let's take that Gentile co-worker you won for the Lord at lunch to your messianic synagogue and see how well he fairs. The service is Friday night, so he has to hurry home from work. He enters the building and a *Shamash* (usher) hands him a Shabbat siddur and wishes him "Shabbat shalom." As the service starts, most of the people jump to the empty spaces in the room for some Israeli style dance and celebration—not exactly what he experienced at the Episcopal Church growing up! In between songs, there are more prayers and blessings spoken in Hebrew, and they are reading from the back of the book forward! (Hebrew Bibles read right to left.) Banners and flags, prayer shawls and kippahs, dancing and Hebrew—*wow… don't these people ever just sit down and be quiet for two minutes?* (If many of the terms used in this last paragraph are unfamiliar to you, then I guess I just made my point very nicely!)

So how on earth are we ever going to reconcile these two worlds and become one big happy family? Are we all supposed to worship the same way with the same traditions, prayers, and expressions? Or were we intended to be a large family from every nation, tribe, and tongue? Were we indeed created to love and respect each other, and enjoy our differences, while supporting the commonalities of our faith? I must say, after over three decades of ministry work and having visited over seventy nations, I have come to enjoy, and even celebrate, our differences in cultures and styles, while holding to the truths which make us *all* a family in His Kingdom.

Father, May They Be One

Let's take a look at Scripture in John 17. These well-known verses find Yeshua praying for three distinct groups, just before He is arrested and crucified. First, He prayed for Himself, as He was well aware of the terrifying experience He was about to endure for the salvation of Israel and the entire world. Second, He prayed for the disciples—for their strength, protection, joy, and unity. And finally, He prayed for all those who would believe in Him through the testimony of the disciples— you, me, and the millions who have placed their eternal trust in Jesus' sacrifice and even those who are yet to believe. Listen again to the heart of Jesus as He prays for the unity of us all:

> *My prayer is not for them alone. I pray also for those who will believe in me through their message, that all of them may be one, Father, just as you are in me and I am in you. May they also be in us so that the world may believe that you have sent me. I have given them the glory that you gave me, that they may be one as we are one: I in them and you in me. May they be brought to complete unity to let the world know that you sent me and have loved them even as you have loved me.*
>
> —John 17:20-23

Jesus' intentions here are crystal clear, don't you think? He prayed for the unity of all believers, down through the ages because this *One New Man* would be the greatest testimony of the claim of His messiahship before the world. More than His healing miracles, more than the words He spoke, even more than the sign of Lazarus raised from the dead, the unity of Jews and Gentiles in Him is *the proof* of His right to sit on the throne of David. Incredible!

Now, how is this accomplished? He told us clearly in His prayer: by giving us the glory that God gave to Him. It is *His glory* that gives us the power to walk and live in the kind of unity for which He prayed. We don't have the ability, in and of ourselves to do this. We must rely on the glory of God to do the work for us. It is our unity with Him, first of all, which gives us the power to live in unity with one another. This is where the

Without *oneness with Yeshua* as individuals, there is no glory to bind us all together in Him.

glory comes from! Notice in Jesus' prayer how He first points out His unity with the Father as the prerequisite for the unity of the whole body of believers. In other words, without *oneness with Yeshua* as individuals, there is no glory to bind us all together in Him. We need His glory to live as this One New Man!

Behold How Good...

In the Psalms, King David revealed his amazement at the resulting glory from God's people living in unity. In Psalm 133, David wrote:

> *How good and pleasant it is when brothers dwell together in unity!*
> *It is like precious oil poured on the head, running down on the beard,*
> *running down on Aaron's beard, down upon the collar of his robes.*
> *It is as if the dew of Hermon were falling on Mount Zion.*
> *For there the Lord bestows his blessing, even life forevermore.*

Notice the last word of the first sentence—*unity*. It is the Hebrew word *echad,* meaning *one.* In the 1960s, a group called Three Dog Night sang, "One is the loneliest number that you'll ever do." But here, due to context, David is not talking about the lonely *one*, but rather a unity resulting from many in one (as in a cluster of grapes). In the Hebrew, it is rendered as *eshkol echad*, one cluster. Isn't that a beautiful way to think about this unity? We are one cluster, having many members. We are all unique in size, color, flavor, and more, yet still one cluster—together—all being nourished by the One True Vine.

As I considered this verse, reading it in Hebrew, I really wanted the translation to read a little differently. Because of the prayer of Jesus in John 17: 20-23, I wanted the last line to translate as: *For there the Lord bestows His glory* (in order to make a powerful point to all of this). But I realized that it was the glory given to us that enables us to walk in this unity in the first place! So when we walk in the glory, which brings unity and displays to the world that Yeshua is the Messiah, there He adds, or bestows, or commands, his *b'racha*, or blessing, which brings life forevermore! Selah on that thought for a few minutes.

I have read a wonderful description of the word *blessing*. It can mean: *endued by God with power for success, prosperity, long life, and fruit that remains*. How's that for being blessed? Unity, glory, blessing, life forevermore! Come on, who wouldn't want all of that? And it all comes from the Lord as we walk together as the One New Man, Jew and Gentile together. Hallelujah!

So how do we achieve—or even aspire—to all of this, as we come from so many different backgrounds, traditions, and worship styles? Now isn't that the ten million dollar question? I believe the key word for us today concerning this is *humility*. Can we enjoy each other's uniqueness without thinking everyone should worship the way we do? Can we be mature enough to kneel, with our denominational brothers and sisters, receive the wafer, or sing "Shout to the Lord" with our Pentecostal and charismatic brothers? Can we recite the Sh'ma with our messianic brothers during a Torah service, and still not fall off the Vine? You know what happens to grapes that become separated from the vine, don't you? They shrivel up, die, and end up surrounded by a whole bunch of bran flakes!

It is the glory of God that enables us to have this unity, love, faith, and grace. In fact, if we cannot operate in unity, then I believe I can say on good authority—there is no glory present. The Hebrew word for glory is *kavod*, meaning *the weight of His presence*. So in light of this, consider this sobering statement:

No humility, no presence. No presence, no glory.
No glory, no unity nor blessing.
No blessing, no One New Man.
Where there is no One New Man,
there is no testimony of Jesus the Messiah!

We had better get this truth down, deep inside of our souls. Could this be one of the major reasons why faith in Europe is at an all-time low? It is estimated that only about two percent of that entire continent are true Bible believers today. Could it be that the devastation of the Holocaust and the silence of the Church have so broken the unity of this One New Man that it has left behind no presence, no glory, and no testimony of the Kingship of Jesus in much of Europe?

This is a very sobering thought to me and has become more important than my "little" ways of doing things or how I prefer to worship. We are one cluster, one body. There is only One Lord and Savior of us ALL—Jesus Christ—Yeshua the Messiah. So let us humble ourselves, and worship Him together in spirit and in truth. May the glory return, bringing unity, which invites the blessing and the testimony of Yeshua!

And They Sang...

It occurred to me, if we want to know what this One New Man, or Kingdom man, looks like, sounds like, and worships like, it is very helpful to get a sneak-peek into the throne room of heaven. These glimpses into heavenly worship are few-and-far between in Scripture.

Revelation, chapter 15, speaks of a time yet to come, but it gives us the lyrics to a very interesting song of worship used in heaven. Let me simply quote the Scriptures here, and you will immediately understand:

And I saw what looked like a sea of glass mixed with fire and, standing beside the sea, those who had been victorious over the beast and his image, and over the number of his name. They held harps given them by God and sang the song of Moses the servant of God and the song of the Lamb:

Great and marvelous are your deeds, Lord God Almighty.
Just and true are your ways, King of the Ages.
Who will not fear you,
O Lord, and bring glory to your name?
For you alone are holy.
All nations will come and worship before you, for your righteous acts have been revealed.
—Revelation 15:3-4

Isn't it interesting that in heavenly worship they still sing the song of Moses? Why would they sing that when the Lamb is right there in their midst? This actually makes perfect sense for several reasons. One good reason has already been stated earlier—the Bible is one continuous revelation to One People of God, one Kingdom made up of Jews and Gentiles, those who love and worship the King.

The song of Moses is a revelation of the One True God of heaven and earth. He is great, marvelous, just, and true. The song is a revelation of the Kingdom, its Law, and its King. It reveals the foundation for the workings of the Kingdom and its people. It speaks of the glory of the Kingdom past, present, and future, and declares the coming of the King of the Kingdom. In fact, without the song of Moses, there would be no song of the Lamb!

CHAPTER 5

Reconciling the King's Laws

The Kingdom Extends to the Uttermost Parts

Yeshua did not come to the earth to announce the start of the second great monotheistic religion. Instead, He came as the Promised One of Israel, the Anointed, the Messiah, and He came preaching the Kingdom of God, to the Jew first, then to the Gentile (Rom. 1:16).

After His resurrection, standing on the Mount of Olives, Yeshua made it abundantly clear that this Kingdom was to be preached from Jerusalem to the uttermost parts of the earth (Acts 1:8). This was such a foreign concept to Jesus' Jewish followers that even then His intentions had to be clarified and confirmed by supernatural signs and wonders. We see this in both the supernatural conversion and calling of Saul of Tarsus, renamed the Paul in Acts 9 and with Peter in his vision in Acts 10.

The prophet Isaiah clearly spoke about the expansion of the Kingdom into all the earth. Speaking of the Servant of the Lord, Isaiah said,

*I will keep you and will make you to be a covenant for the
people [Israel] and a light for the Gentiles [Nations].*
                                                    —Isaiah 42:6b

*It is too small a thing for you to be my servant to restore the
tribes of Jacob and bring back those of Israel I have kept.
I will also make you a light for the Gentiles, that you may
bring my salvation to the ends of the earth.*
                                                    —Isaiah 49:6

These words from Isaiah made a foundation for the well-known
declaration of the apostle John in his gospel:

*For God so loved the world that he gave his one and only
Son, that whoever believes in him shall not perish but have
eternal life.*
                                                    —John 3:16

The Law and the Kingdom Today

Even though Jesus is the Savior of the world and wants the
Kingdom to expand to the uttermost parts of the earth, He never
advocated, nor did He indicate in the least, some kind of cataclysmic
separation from the faith of Abraham, Isaac, and Jacob (later called
Israel). To the contrary, He promised that as long as there remains the
sun, moon, and stars, He would not cast away His people Israel (Jer.
31:35-37). In fact, He affirmed this faith and declared, "For truly I tell
you, until heaven and earth disappear, not the smallest letter, not the
least stroke of a pen, will by any means disappear from the Law until
everything is accomplished" (Matt. 5:18).

What is the *Law*? Law, or Torah, is defined in the Kohlenberger
dictionary as "instruction, regulation, and doctrine." The word used
by Yeshua Himself in Matthew and Luke is the Greek word *nomos,*
meaning "law, principle, rule; most frequently, the divine Law given

by Moses, whether moral, ceremonial or judicial."

So how should we, New Covenant believers, approach the Torah (generally referring to the first five books of the Old Testament)? Are the writings of the prophets and the historical books important for us today? I believe the Tanakh, or Old Testament, is absolutely essential and foundational for our understanding of who God is—His ways, His laws, and His precepts. It provides a full scope of His plans for Christians, for Israel, the nations, and the Kingdom to come. Who is the Messiah, how will we know Him, and what will He do? All this, and more, is contained within the Old Testament.

So am I also saying that we should carefully comb through these Scriptures and find every law to obey? What about the 613 Jewish laws? My intention here is not to get bogged down in teaching Torah, but simply to establish the Tanakh as the foundation for our faith. We should appreciate it in the light of the New Covenant and the inspiration of the Ruach HaKodesh—the Holy Spirit—who guides us to all truth.

Many times, over the years, when I have shared these things with people, I get the response, "But we are not under the law anymore, brother; we are under grace!" Listen, I am the first one to stand up and shout "Hallelujah!" for the grace of God. But if you think we have somehow been freed from the responsibility of God's morality, from His ways and precepts, then we are not on the same page.

My friend, and internationally respected author and speaker John Bevere, made a powerful statement about grace that I will never forget. He said that "grace was not God's power to forgive sin, but rather grace was God's divine power working in us to *overcome* sin! So the whole concept of *sloppy agape* or grace for willful sinning has no real foundation in any kind of truth."

Look at what the prophet Jeremiah wrote regarding the coming of the promised New Covenant: "The time is coming," declares the Lord, "when I will make a new covenant with the house of Israel and the house of Judah...I will put my law [TORAH] in their minds and write it on their hearts. I will be their God and they will be my people" (Jer. 31:31, 33b).

The prophet Ezekiel was just as clear about the New Covenant:

I will give you a new heart and put a new spirit in you; I will remove from you your heart of stone and give you a heart of flesh. And I will put my Spirit in you and move you to follow my decrees and be careful to keep my laws.
—Ezekiel 36:26-27

I think some of the teachings we have heard with regards to these important things should cause us to reflect. The New Covenant is not to be taken as a license to disobey God or to continue in willful sin. Jesus came and gave us His Spirit. He has written the laws of God upon our hearts and minds, through the new birth. He put His Spirit in us that we may live in righteousness and live morally.

Having said all this, I find it intriguing that there is so much more interest in the teaching of Jewish "roots" and practices today than ever before. As a result, there is more messianic praise and worship music, more travel to Israel, and more conferences. There are even more messianic congregations in the United States, and in Israel herself, than at any other time in history. Could all this be a sign of things to come?

The Fulfillment of the Law in the Kingdom Today

Many will lump all the writings and instruction of the Tanakh (Old Testament) into one big dismissible lump and call it: LAW. This is a huge mistake. The Tanakh, or Hebrew Bible, is actually divided into three distinct sections: the Torah, the Prophets, and the Writings (or historical books). Each section has distinct value for us today. In 1 Corinthians 10, Paul refers to the Old Testament warnings written for our counsel.

In the book of Matthew (chapters 5-7), Jesus sat down on a beautiful hillside, overlooking the Sea of Galilee and began to teach what has become known as the *Sermon on the Mount*. Let me direct your attention to an interesting verse here. In Matthew 5, verse 17,

Yeshua stated, "Do not think that I have come to abolish the Law or the Prophets; I have not come to abolish them but to fulfill them."

The word I find to be misunderstood here, quite often, is "fulfilled." What is the first thing that comes to your mind when you hear the word *fulfilled*? I believe most people think of *passed away* or *a task completed*. But this is not at all what is meant by the Greek word "plero-o" (used by Yeshua in the Sermon on the Mount). Rather, it means "filled to the full," or "to fully satisfy." It is more accurate, then, to define the word *fulfill* as "to raise to its highest expression."

So in the Sermon on the Mount, which could quite accurately be called the New Covenant Torah, Jesus plainly explained what He meant as He continued saying, "You have heard that it was said to the people long ago, 'Do not murder, and anyone who murders will be subject to judgment.' But I tell you that anyone who is angry with his brother will be subject to judgment" (Matt. 5:21-22). He continued and said, "You have heard that it was said, 'Do not commit adultery.' But I tell you that anyone who looks at a woman lustfully has already committed adultery with her in his heart" (Matt. 5:27-28).

Does this still sound like *passed away*, *done away with* or *irrelevant* to you? No, it sounds more like *beyond possible to keep*! And that is exactly why our righteousness, or right standing with God, is based on Yeshua's blood and not our own works or deeds! However, this does not get us off the hook from our responsibility to walk in the ways, precepts, and laws of the God we serve. In fact, one of the ministries of the Holy

One of the ministries of the Holy Spirit in us is to convict us of the Law written on our hearts, and lead us in paths of righteousness for His name's sake.

Spirit in us is to convict us of the *Law* written on our hearts, and lead us in paths of righteousness for His name's sake. In his early ministry, the apostle Paul argued this very point to a carnal group in Rome. They thought: *Since we are under grace, it really doesn't matter how we live.*

We are going to heaven anyway! If that were true, then we wouldn't need the provision of the power of the blood of Jesus to call upon when we do sin! Again, the apostle Paul answered this question of law versus faith and grace when he asked, "Do we, then, nullify the law by this faith? Not at all! Rather, we uphold the law" (Rom. 3:31).

So when we pray and ask Yeshua to be the Lord of our life, we are born again and become a new creation (2 Cor. 5:17). We, therefore, want to please Him in all our ways. Our heart now declares to us: *Love the Lord your God with all your heart, soul, strength and might...Serve the Lord with gladness...Come before His presence with singing...Love your neighbor as yourself...Don't take what isn't yours...Apologize for unkind words...Guard your eyes and ears...Protect your heart...Take captive every thought to obey the mind of Messiah.*

In short, what happened to us when we believed and asked Yeshua to be the Lord of our life is that the Ruach HaKodesh—the Holy Spirit—came and wrote His New Covenant Torah on our hearts. Then, He took up residency in us as the temple of God. He continually guides, corrects, teaches, admonishes, and leads us into all the truth. Amazing! It's a mystery, and yet absolutely true.

Free From the Law of Sin and Death

So what did the sacrifice of the Messiah actually free us from? We were freed from *the law of sin and death*. And what exactly is this law we have avoided by faith in Yeshua? This law, which hung over all our heads, is most clearly defined for us by the prophet Ezekiel (18:20) when he declared, "The soul who sins is the one who will die." He states this truth again in chapter thirty-three, as does Jeremiah (31:30), the writer of 2 Kings 14:6, and the apostle Paul in Romans 6:23 when he stated, "For the wages of sin is death." The problem, which we all have in common, is that "[we] all have sinned and fall short of the glory of God" (Rom. 3:23). How disturbing! We *all* have sinned, and the soul that sins must die. That's a *no win* situation.

The great part about all of this is that Jehovah had the prescription for our victory over sin laid out since the Garden of Eden. Even when He was cursing the serpent and handing out judgment to Adam and Eve for high treason, Jesus was already in place to come crush the serpent's head. The Devil's days were numbered!

We are no longer under the law of sin and death because we already died with Yeshua and His law is written on our hearts with grace that gives us power over sin and death. No human has ever been declared righteous because of his or her own deeds. Even Isaiah says *all* our righteousness is as filthy rags in God's sight (Isa. 64:4-7), but it is the blood of the Lamb of God that makes us righteous. We do what we do to please Him, not to obtain favor, righteousness, or salvation. In Galatians it says that "by the law shall no flesh be justified." So having been set free from the law of sin and death, made alive with Messiah, now that we walk in His grace, which gives us power over sin, and having been clothed in His righteousness, filled with the same Spirit that raised Jesus from the dead (Rom. 8:11), what about all the rules and regulations? Am I *required* to obey them all?

This is an important question and one that deserves an answer that is more than just a trivial quip. In my travels and experiences, I still see a lot of confusion among true believers, those who sincerely desire to please God. Some simply dismiss the question of obedience to God's laws with the typical, "Jesus freed us from all that." Yet, others get so caught up in their desire to live a "Torah-observant life" that they live like legalistic Ultra-Orthodox Jews.

I have asked my dear friend of over three decades, Asher Intrater, to weigh in on this subject. Asher Intrater is the founder and apostolic leader of Revive Israel Ministries, and oversees Ahavat Yeshua Congregation in Jerusalem, and Tiferet Yeshua Congregation in Tel Aviv. Asher was one of the founders of Tikkun International, and serves on the board of the Messianic Alliance of Israel and Aglow International. He has been living and ministering in Israel for more than twenty years, with his wife, Betty, and their four children. He is a pastor, author, teacher, and a covenant friend, whose life and worldwide ministry has impacted many. The next chapter will include his teaching on this subject.

CHAPTER 6

God's Harmony
of the Law and Grace

This first section is taken, with permission, entirely from Asher
Intrater's newsletter dated February, 2009.

The Ladder of Gospel and Law by Asher Intrater

The relationship between the Gospel message and
Jewish tradition can be described in a simple way by
imagining a ladder of four rungs or priorities:

- salvation by grace
- moral law
- ritual law
- religious tradition

Salvation by Grace

Yeshua took our punishment on the cross and then
rose from the dead to provide eternal life. That message
is more important than anything else. We are beings
created by a loving and holy God. We all have sinned; all
righteousness comes from Him, and...without trusting in

His righteousness, no human being can hope to become righteous on his own. That is the central theme of the book of Romans and an eternal truth that is beyond dispute.

Moral Law

For that reason, salvation by grace is more important than the moral Law; yet moral standards are essential. And who establishes what those standards are... only one who himself is perfectly righteous! Therefore, moral standards must come from God alone. God's moral standards are absolute and valid for all human beings. They are written in the Bible. The most succinct list of His moral code is the Ten Commandments. (See Matthew 19:17)

Within the Law are commandments of greater importance, and those of lesser importance. Yeshua exhorted us not to "forsake the weightier matters of the Law, i.e. justice, mercy and faith" (Matthew 23:23). In order to obey God's commandments, we have to understand which aspects are more important, and which less important.

Ritual Law

The basic division between what is primary and what is secondary is between the moral law (love) and the ritual law (symbols). "To love God with all your heart and all your understanding and all your might, and to love your neighbor as yourself, behold, is greater than all sacrifice and offering" (Mark 12:30).

Ritual laws or "signs" of the covenant are not binding commandments in the same way that the moral commandments are. "Neither circumcision nor uncircumcision is important, but rather keeping the commandments of God" (I Corinthians 7:19). Isn't circumcision a commandment? Yes, in the sense that it is part of the ritual law recorded in the Bible. No, in the sense that it is not part of the absolute moral law.

Circumcision, festivals, and food laws are not on the same level as the commandments against lying, stealing, adultery, and murder. Not recognizing the priority of moral law over ritual law is a critical misunderstanding of the Law itself, and may result in religious hypocrisy. Yeshua rebuked the Pharisees for misinterpreting and therefore disobeying the Law. "Woe to you, blind guides, who strain a gnat and swallow a camel" (Matthew 23:24). (Unfortunately, much of the Christian world has rejected the Law altogether, often resulting in sin and moral transgression even by those who preach the gospel.)

Religious Tradition

The ritual aspects of Jewish law may be divided into two sections: those that are biblical, and those which are additions from the rabbis. The symbols in the Bible are specifically ordained by God with a spiritual message concerning His kingdom plan. Those added by the rabbis are a matter of culture and have no direct authority.

Elevating tradition to the status of divine law is extremely dangerous. Yeshua referred to this as "the learned commandment of men" (quoting Isaiah 29:13), and asked, "Why do you disobey the commandment of God for the sake of your own traditions?" (Matthew

15:3). Equating religious tradition to the Law of God is an evil found in all religion, whether Jewish, Christian, or pagan.

Religious tradition is never binding. However, when we share the good news of salvation, we should embrace in love the culture of the people group we are sharing with. This is particularly true of the Jewish people, who developed a religious culture based on Old Testament.(Tenakh). "For the sake of the Jews, I am as a Jew in order to win them [for salvation]; for the sake of those under the Law, I am as one under the Law" (I Corinthians 9:20).

In summary:

- The message of salvation through Yeshua is our highest priority.
- Good works of human origin cannot save us.
- God's absolute moral law is binding for all human beings.
- Moral law is higher than ritual law.
- Biblical symbols or rituals point to spiritual kingdom truths.
- Religious tradition is never binding or authoritative.
- Elevating religious tradition to moral law is a dangerous error.
- Embracing someone else's culture in love may be an important bridge in sharing with them eternal life.

Apples of Gold

Think of this biblical parable: "Apples of gold in

settings of silver is a word spoken in its fashions" (Proverbs 25:11).

What we have to say is compared to a golden apple. How we say it is compared to fittings of silver. We in the Messianic movement have often been so concerned with the Jewish form of what we have to say, that we miss the center of the message itself. Our Jewish culture and identity is not the message. Sometimes we have offered a silver setting without the golden apple. On the other hand, the setting is important. If a Frenchman wanted to give an Englishman a fish, he might write on the box "poisson" (French for "fish"). However, the Englishman would undoubtedly think it was "poison." Often well-meaning Christians have tried to bring the "fish" of eternal life to our people, yet our people see it as poison.

We want to have the right message and the right manner of expression; the right content in the right context: the gospel of Yeshua in its Jewish historical setting is what we seek to restore and live out, governed by the Law of love and the revelation of the Holy Spirit.

—Asher Intrater

Messianic Law

If you have been around for a while, searching with your antennas up, you have undoubtedly, come across some groups of messianic believers who say very different things on this subject. One group is called One Law, and they believe that all followers of Jesus — Jew or Gentile — are called to keep the entire Law. I believe this an erroneous view, which stands against even a simple reading of Acts 15, and it brings confusion to the Church.

Another group is called the Ephraimites (or Two Houses, or Two

Sticks). This group teaches that all believers are descendants of Israel—Jewish believers from the tribe of Judah and everyone else belong to one of the ten lost tribes. Again, there are many problems with this teaching, and it also is a source of confusion. Needless to say, I am of neither of these persuasions.

My friend, Dr. Daniel C. Juster, has written extensively on these groups and should be a help to you if you desire further study. His papers can be found on the website of the Union of Messianic Jewish Congregations (www.UMJC.org).

A YouTube™ Revelation! — *A Spirit-Filled Revelation*

During the time I was praying and writing about these things, I came upon a video that cleared up a lot of confusion for me in just three and a half minutes! It's the story of Stacy Westfall and her now famous championship ride in the freestyle reining event at the 2006 All American Quarter Horse Congress. The audience wasn't prepared for what Stacy brought to the show that day. It has captured the hearts of all who have witnessed the incredible bond of trust and love displayed.

Reining, according to Wikipedia, is a western riding competition for horses where the riders guide the horse through a precise pattern of circles, spins, and stops. The horse must be responsive to its rider, willingly guided and controlled with little or no resistance. In a standard competition, the horse and rider enter the arena and go through an entire routine to display the horsemanship and training of the two. What made Stacy's routine so unusual was that her horse was not wearing a saddle, bit, reins, or a bridle! The audience watched almost spellbound as the two went through a flawless routine with only the rider's voice guiding the horse. As I watched the video, my heart was rejoicing

The Law, written upon our hearts, draws us to His grace, as we desire to obey His voice and walk in His ways.

at the display. But then I heard the Lord whisper to me…*That's what happened when you were born again. You traded the bit and bridle of an exterior code for a loving rider who has trained you with a loving voice.*

His words stunned me! But as I considered what I had just heard and seen on the video, it all began to come into focus for me. You see, with a carnal, unregenerate spirit, we need the bit, bridle, and reins of the external code (Law) to guide and direct us, and even sometimes to force us into obedience. But when we are born from above, the laws are written on our hearts, and the voice of the Rider guides and directs our life.

So in this metaphor, we are the horse, and the training we undergo—with the saddle, reins, bit, and bridle— is the Law. But when we surrender to the Gospel of the King, the Rider—the Holy Spirit— leads and guides us to the Truth. I love this analogy, as it puts the whole thing in perspective for me. This example also leaves room for the Spirit of God to train me differently than He trains you. The important thing is that we are listening to the voice of the Rider!

Take a moment to search "Stacy Westfall Championship Run 2006" on the internet and see if you don't get goose bumps like I did. Let the Holy Spirit speak to you as He did to me.

A Heart to Obey the King of the Kingdom

The Kingdom of God is not a list of *do's* and *don'ts*, which we obey with a bit and bridle in our mouths. Neither have the laws of God and His Kingdom been *replaced* by grace. But rather, the Law, written upon our hearts, draws us *to* His grace, as we *desire* to obey His voice and walk in His ways. And His blood is readily available to us when we do transgress from His ways. It removes our sin, that we may be forgiven and cleansed from all unrighteousness (1 John 1:9). We have also been set free from the *curse of the law* that states the soul that sins *must* die. This is why the New Covenant is a better covenant, with better promises. In other words, those things which the written code was unable to accomplish have now been *fulfilled* by the indwelling of the Spirit—the same Spirit who raised Jesus from the dead—the Holy Spirit, the Ruach HaKodesh! And isn't it amazing that we celebrate both the giving of the Law and the giving of the Spirit on the same day—the Feast of the Lord...Shavuot (pronounced *shah-voo-ote*), Pentecost, the Feast of Weeks. (Lev. 23, Joel 2, Acts 2)

CHAPTER 7

God's Purpose in the Feasts

God's Kingdom and Its History

In today's New Covenant society, when speaking about the Law, Old Testament, Torah, and such, it becomes necessary to state why the feasts are celebrated, while other things are not necessarily adhered to. Why celebrate Passover, but not stone someone for adultery or breaking the Sabbath? What about the purity laws? Why not boycott restaurants that serve pork and shellfish?

We do not live in a religious society or a theocracy, but rather, we live in a secular society that has rebelled against God and His ways. One day Messiah Yeshua will return to the earth, and He will rule and reign from Jerusalem. He will judge the nations and put all things back in order. He will even withhold rain from nations that will not come to Jerusalem to celebrate the Feast of Tabernacles (Zech. 14). Christians are *in* this world, but we are not to be a part *of* it. We are members of a different Kingdom—a Kingdom whose Maker and Ruler is God Himself. So while living here, we experience the tension of rendering unto Caesar what is Caesar's and unto God what is God's.

There are only two kingdoms in the universe—the kingdom of darkness, ruled by Satan—and the Kingdom of God, ruled by Adonai

(Hebrew word for LORD, which means owner and ruler of all) with Yeshua as King of Kings. Every kingdom has a history, or events, worth remembering and celebrating. In fact, in ancient Israel, the Lord commanded that national celebrations be remembered, and observed by everyone, three times a year. These celebrations are foundational events of the Kingdom, as well as great victories by the King of the Kingdom, worthy of recognition *and* celebration. They are significant as historical fact, important today for our daily lives, *and* they contain *not yet fulfilled* elements of prophetic insight and hope for the future.

The Passover of Exodus will have a future fulfillment when the Jewish population, from *all* nations, is gathered back to Israel. Shavuot, or Pentecost, will have a greater fulfillment when all our sons and daughters prophesy. The tabernacles will have a huge impact on the globe when the last great harvest of souls takes place (from every tribe, tongue, people and nation). The Torah is the foundation for all Scripture, and anything that comes after it must agree with what is written there. The holy days, the cycles and rhythms of nature, and our own lives find a divine pattern instituted for our good, not to merely bind us up into some pattern of religious obedience. The entire universe was established by the spoken word of the living God, and He also set into each time and season a rhythm for work, play, rest and worship. Yeshua observed these very same rhythms and cycles, and He taught His disciples to do the same.

Is it *mandatory* for every believer to keep the feasts and celebrate the goodness and promises of God? No. We have the liberty to eat, work, and even smoke ourselves into an early grave. We can be sickly, obese, distraught, exhausted, and of no earthy use to God, or mankind, if we choose to be. But is that the abundant life that Jesus came to secure for us? Absolutely not!

So, you are a Christian, Jesus is Lord of your life, you are born again into the Kingdom of God, Christ is your King, and now you want to be more like Him, right? Well, He said, "If you obey my word [Law, commandments], then you are truly my disciples" (John 8:31). Jesus also said in John 5:19 that He did *only* what He saw His Father do.

Then, it would stand to reason, since Jesus celebrated the feasts of the Lord, that He saw His Father celebrate them!

Jesus is the fullness and the reason for the feasts of the spring. He is the Lamb of the Passover. His blood is the fullness of deliverance and forgiveness, which is now applied to the doorposts of the hearts of men. He is the first fruits of those who are raised from the dead through faith (in Him!). He is the giver of the Law and the giver of the Holy Spirit on Shavuot/Pentecost. And when He returns…it will be at the sounding of a shofar from heaven, Yom T'ruah (Rosh HaShanah). Israel will mourn for Him as an only son (Yom Kippur). He will gather the harvest of souls of the nations—Sukkot (Tabernacles)!

He is the King of the Kingdom. He is the living Rock who provided for Israel in the desert. He is the living Word on Mount Sinai and the Mount of Beatitudes. He is the King who is soon to come. He will appear at the sound of the shofar. He is both Israel's Son and Savior. He is the Gatherer of the harvest and the Judge of the nations, the Lion of the tribe of Judah, the Glory of His people Israel and the Light of all the nations.

He is our victory and the reason we gather together to celebrate!

Many Kingdom people today, especially if they are not Jewish, do not see these celebrations as part of their own history. Therefore, they don't identify with the covenant people who came thousands of years before them. Jews, on the other hand, are instructed to retell the story of Passover each year to their children, as if they had actually come out of Egypt along with their ancestors.

For some Christians, there is a very real and palpable intertestamental period, with a complete disconnect from the Torah, or Old Testament writings. Many Gentile Christians begin reading the Bible in Matthew. They struggle to identify with Israel, the Kingdom, and the Jewish people. Even identifying Jesus as a Jewish rabbi is a stretch for some. This is one reason why the statement of Ruth, the Moabite, is so powerful. She not only embraced the God of Israel, but she also identified with the people, the land, the calendar of feasts and celebrations, and the destiny of the Kingdom for the Jewish people. In fact, it was this wholehearted embrace that won her a place of honor in the history of the Kingdom and the very lineage of Messiah himself! She celebrated the Feast of Shavuot (Pentecost), won the heart of Boaz, and secured a seat in the House of the Lord Jesus, King of the Jews. Let's read what Ruth said to Naomi when she was encouraged to go back to her own people and land:

> *Don't urge me to leave you or to turn back from you. Where you go I will go, and where you stay I will stay. Your people will be my people and your God my God. Where you die I will die, and there I will be buried. May the LORD deal with me, be it ever so severely, if even death separates you and me." When Naomi realized that Ruth was determined to go with her, she stopped urging her.*
>
> —Ruth 1:16-18

Don't Move The Ancient Stones!

"Do not move an ancient boundary stone set up by your forefathers" (Proverbs 22:28).

It struck me immediately after reading this verse that this is exactly what we have done with regards to the Law, the Feasts of the Lord, and the Word of God—all to our great harm. We have embraced many of the traditions of men rather than the words of our God. We have moved the ancient stones to redefine the Kingdom in our own terms and through the eyes of our own culture, making good-sounding excuses for the repositioning of the borders.

We have embraced many of the traditions of men rather than the words of our God. We have moved the ancient stones to redefine the Kingdom in our own terms and through the eyes of our own culture, making good-sounding excuses for the repositioning of the borders. And what have we used as a guide or plumb line for these moves? We have used culture, expedience, convenience, and *the ways*

that seem right to a man—almost anything but the traditions of our fathers and the Word of the living God! So it raises the question: *Who are the fathers we are now following?*

If you listen carefully you can almost hear the ranting of the Roman Emperor Constantine, as he forbids any prayers, hymns, readings, celebrations, songs, or traditions of the Jews. Constantine may have thought: *Let them have their empty religion, but we—the Church of Rome—have better ideas and better holidays to ascribe to the works of God.*

I realize some of these things may be uncomfortable to deal with. This may not be something you have concerned yourself with or even thought about. We have well-entrenched celebrations in the West with some godly stones in their foundation, but they have also taken on the wood, hay, and stubble of our liberal society and culture. In fact, some have been so completely removed from their original place and practices, they can't even be remotely recognized as either historically Biblical or godly.

The Easter holiday is a perfect example. The purpose and intention of the holiday is to celebrate the resurrection of Jesus, King of the Jews, from the dead. So why did we need to move the historical date and rename the feast after a Babylonian queen/goddess when we already had the Feast of First Fruits? What is wrong with Passover, Unleavened Bread, and First Fruits—the feasts which Jehovah chose to reveal His Lamb, who would take away our sins? With all due respect, is Jesus the Passover Lamb or the Easter ham? So we now have a *holy day* named after Nimrod's adulterous wife, celebrated with the painting of chicken eggs, wearing of bonnets, eating chocolate bunnies and marshmallow eggs, and a "traditional" dinner featuring a baked ham… *terrific*! But what in the world does any of this have to do with Yeshua, the Kingdom, salvation, or anything else for that matter? Has anyone else asked these questions?

Does anybody really know what time it is…does anybody really care? Yes, I have borrowed a line from one of my favorite rock groups from the sixties and seventies, Chicago Transit Authority (later shortened to simply *Chicago).* Some churches, of late, have ceased to use the term *Easter* and opted for the term *Resurrection Sunday,* in order to address this dilemma. But why not just surrender to the biblical model and be done with it? What is the problem here?

Do pastors not know, do they not care, or are they afraid that something so radical as embracing the Calendar of the Kingdom will lose them a sizable number of bodies in their weekly worship services? I don't wish to be harsh or mean spirited here, and I do understand the pressures of culture and tradition. I really believe there is a better way for us Kingdom folk and if you read on you will discover what I am talking about.

PART 2

CHAPTER 8

The Calendar of His Kingdom

The Calendar of the Kingdom

And now—the case for *Embracing the Calendar of the Kingdom!*

[WARNING: I am going to make some bold statements regarding the Calendar of God's Kingdom, but I want you to know up front, these are *not* commandments, but rather, they are invitations to grace and understanding. I would never support putting feasts in front of who the feast represents.]

Any kingdom, no matter how large or small, will have a story to tell—its beginnings, history, and journey through time. There will be stories about the earliest pioneers, and the sacrifices they made to carry out their vision. There will be good times and bad times, of course, as well as losses along side great victories, which helped shape and fashion the kingdom as it exists today. These events may be seen as national celebrations, such as Independence Day on the 4th of July and Thanksgiving Day in the United States. These are historical events that helped shape our past, link us together as a people, and speak about our future as a nation.

Along with these major celebrations, there are also some of

lesser importance that get varying degrees of attention from the public. American holidays such as Labor Day and Columbus Day might fit this description, but they are a part of the fabric of a nation, and rightly have a place in the calendar of national celebrations. These celebrations, no matter how important some may perceive them to be, are not required to be observed in order to be a citizen of this country. By this, I mean that no one will be arrested if they don't attend a fireworks display on the 4th of July. You will not be deported to your grandparent's country of origin if you don't display an American flag on Memorial Day, and so forth. But many of these celebrations, or feasts, mark periods of great challenge and victory by the citizens who have gone before us. I would dare to say, they deserve some degree of observance simply because we are citizens of the United States of America.

Consider this then: We who are a part of the Kingdom of God share a common history with all those who have gone before us. The book of Genesis is just as much a part of our history as is the gospel of John. Whether we are Jew or Gentile, male or female, black or white, the Bible calls us all the seed of Abraham and heirs according to the promise by faith. Our Sovereign Lord has gone to great lengths to record, and preserve, our knowledge of this history and to bring us to where we are today. Yeshua prayed that we would be one, as He and the Father are one. He destroyed the wall of partition and the enmity between us and God, through the sacrifice of His own life. For this reason, as part of the Father's family, all of us should want to know our history and celebrate it, as He has revealed for us to do.

God has established a yearly calendar of celebrations, and He invites us to set time aside from our busy lives and come celebrate His past victories over His enemies, who tried to destroy His Kingdom and our families.

Where is this calendar, and why have you not heard about it until now?

Well, the invitation has been extended to all Kingdom citizens for thousands of years. Trouble is, there has evolved a citizenship that is either unaware of this calendar of national celebrations (never having been taught this history and the value of these events), or simply doesn't care. Because you are reading this book, I believe you are a Kingdom citizen who cares about your history and you are curious to learn more.

The Feasts of the Lord

In Leviticus 23 (also Num. 28 and 29), there is a list of major calendar events that are important to the King. They have been listed in chronological order and briefly described for all to see and understand. Much of the discussion, and dissension, about these dates and their relevance began many years ago after the Kingdom was expanded to include the nations (*goyim* in the Hebrew), along with the direct descendants of Abraham, Isaac, and Jacob.

After the first appearing of the great King, Gentile believers began to outnumber Jewish believers in the Church (Jer. 31:31-34; Ezek. 36:24-27). Because this Kingdom and its history were not a part of their former lives, it did not hold the same place of honor in their hearts and minds. And so, slowly but surely, each of the great victories of the King began to lose its importance and relevance to the newer citizens and began to disappear from the memories and celebrations of the Kingdom. But *they never lost their importance to the King.* Some of the new citizens even began to misquote the King Himself by calling these celebrations the *feasts of the Jews* and the *feasts of Israel.* Well, they certainly *are* that, but *more* than that, they are the *Feasts of the Lord.*

I must divert here for just a light moment and tell you what my friend Steve Merkel of Integrity Music has passed on to me. He told me that he really enjoyed working on all the worship recordings with me, and that he had learned so much through our relationship. One day he said, "You know, Paul, I think I've got the whole feast thing down. In fact, I could summarize the entire calendar thing like this: They tried to kill us; God saved us; LET'S EAT!" I get a kick out of that every time he says it. But you know, it's not that far from the truth! The Passover Feast (Israel's celebration of their deliverance from slavery in Egypt through great miracles, signs, and wonders), Purim or Feast of Esther (deliverance from complete annihilation by the evil Haman), and Hanukkah (salvation from the Assyrians and the miracle of the oil) truly are all reminders of how God has saved the Jewish people with great victories, and He wants us to continue to celebrate those victories. So let's eat!

Do you remember what happened years after Yehovah sent Joseph and his family to Egypt in order to save the children of Israel, as well as the lives of millions of Egyptians from the devastating famine? The book of Exodus (1:8 KJV) records the somber words, "Now there arose up a new king over Egypt, which knew not Joseph." This Pharaoh was given the great privilege of guarding and protecting the precious citizens of the kingdom, those who had saved his ancestors many years before. But because he was not a good student in history class, he inflicted the very devastation on his own kingdom which his fathers had escaped by honoring the gift (Joseph) in their midst. How ironic. If Pharaoh had only discerned the kingdom he sheltered, he could have had a very different future!

Celebrations of the King

Let's take a look at these kingdom celebrations and see if there is anything about them that should draw our attention today. They are meticulously listed for us in the book of Leviticus in the twenty-third chapter. Why not put this book aside for just a moment and read that chapter attentively. When you come back, your perspective may have already changed.

Go ahead, I'll wait right here.

SELAH...

Welcome back! Now, I fully realize the first feast mentioned there in Leviticus is the *Sabbath*, but I'm going to "pass-over" (pun intended) to the next feast and come back to the Sabbath later. As it is written, the first shall be last.

The Feasts of Whom?

Let me just remind you of something that was stated a bit earlier, but bears repeating. You have, undoubtedly, heard many times that these Kingdom celebrations are actually called *the Feasts of the Jews*. Some preachers have called them *the Feasts of Israel*, while others have labeled them *the Feasts of the Bible*. This may all sound good and proper, until we go to the words of the King who actually spoke them into existence. Perhaps this is where the confusion lies today and a simple reading of the actual biblical text will help clear it up.

To find out what the King of Israel thinks about these things, let me take you to the Torah. Looking again at the book of Leviticus, chapter 23, we find the Lord speaking to Moses in the second verse when He says, "Speak to the Israelites and say to them: 'These are *my* appointed feasts, the appointed feasts *of the LORD*, which you are to proclaim as sacred assemblies'" (emphasis added). In verse four, He repeats Himself again with regards to Passover, "These are the Lord's appointed feasts..." In verse five, "The Lord's Passover begins..." and in verse six "...the Lord's Feast of Unleavened Bread..." In verse thirty-four, He states again, perhaps for emphasis, "the Lord's Feast of Tabernacles." So we see, first and foremost, these aren't the feasts of Israel, or the Jews, or even of the Bible. They are the *Feasts of the Lord!*

He is a great King who has had great victories, winning every battle in which He has ever engaged! He has never lost a single skirmish, fight, or argument, and they have all been fought on behalf of His people and His Kingdom. Remember what He spoke to Jehoshaphat through the prophet when He said, "For the battle is not yours, but God's" (2 Chron. 20:15). This is *His* Kingdom, and He is well able to defend it from anyone or anything that comes against it, no matter how large or wicked they may be. The citizens of His Kingdom aren't even enlisted into the army to fight for Him. He has created a whole army of warrior angels, equipped with flaming swords, to do the warring on behalf of the King and His citizens. Then, He invites us all, as citizens of His Kingdom, to His table. We get to celebrate with Him the great victories He has won throughout His reign! (Which just so happens to be from everlasting to everlasting!) Who wouldn't want to accept such a gracious offer? So then—*let's celebrate the victories of the King*!

Two Messiahs?

The feasts of the Lord are inherently joined to the life—past, present, and future—of the King and his Kingdom. Because of this, I think it is helpful to digress for just a moment and share some insights from rabbis who lived and wrote before the time of Messiah's first appearing. These were prayerful, thoughtful, and insightful sages, who made some helpful observations, based on the revelation and understanding they had during their lifetime.

In ancient times, some rabbis believed there would appear two Messiahs, at two different points in time. As they read the Scriptures, they saw two separate personalities, who would fulfill two separate missions in the salvation of Israel. There was Mashiach ben David (Messiah, son of David), a warring Messiah who would reign from his throne in Jerusalem, and there was Mashiach ben Yoseph (Messiah, son of Joseph), a suffering, leprous Messiah, who would carry away the sin and sickness of the people.

It's much easier for us in the twenty-first century to look back through history and see how the ancient sages could have arrived at such a conclusion. When it comes to messianic passages, Scripture seems to speak of two different missions, accomplished at different times, and with very different results. The messianic hope of a deliverer King was very much alive in ancient times, as it is today in the lifestyle and liturgy of today's ultra-Orthodox Jews. (In fact, some non-Jews are confused by the lack of support from these religious zealots with regards to the modern State of Israel. Simply put, these folks do not believe that Israel should exist unless the Messiah comes and sets it up in true Orthodox fashion. They see the Israel of today as a work of the hands of secular Zionist extremists, a conspiracy that stands in the path of the true Israel to come.)

These ancient sages were close to the truth. But rather than two Messiahs appearing at two different times, as they had expected, the truth is there is One Messiah who will appear twice, fulfilling the two streams of prophecy of the suffering servant (Jesus on the cross) and the coming King (Jesus at His second coming)! The first time, He would bear our sin and disease. He would then be raised from the dead in order to reappear a second time at the end of the age to establish the Kingdom of God on earth—Messiah King of Israel, King of the Jews, and the Lion of the Tribe of Judah.

So who is the One True Messiah? What do people believe about Him today?

According to some Lubavitch Orthodox, their late rabbi Menachem Schneerson, called *the Rebbe,* was actually the Messiah. He never made this claim about himself. In fact, he refused the accolades and attention he received from admiring students of his teaching. He was the leader of the world's largest and most influential Hasidic sect of our day, yet, he never set foot in the land of Israel! Many of his followers today expect the Rebbe to be raised from the dead in fulfillment of prophecy (Isaiah 53!). They anxiously await this glorious appearing.

I believe the true Messiah to be Jesus Christ—Rabbi Yeshua of Nazareth. He was born of a virgin in Bethlehem, and He lived many years with His family in Nazareth. He was despised and rejected by His brethren, crucified on a Roman cross, and raised from the dead in Jerusalem. He performed so many healing miracles that they cannot be contained in many volumes of books. He fulfilled hundreds of messianic prophecies, and He will return again, at the end of the age to fulfill His role as—the Lion of the tribe of Judah, King of the Jews, and Messiah King over Jerusalem and all the earth.

CHAPTER 9

Celebrate the Past—
The Spring Feasts

Spring Feasts: To Declare a Future Glory

The spring feasts describe the first coming of Yeshua. We remember His deliverance, sacrifice, resurrection, and the outpouring of His Holy Spirit. We celebrate the significant events of the past and His special relationship with His Father.

Passover, Unleavened Bread, and First Fruits: Deliverance for all Mankind

The first great victory of the King is called the *Passover*. It takes place in the springtime, and its focus is on God's marvelous miracles and act of deliverance for His people. The fullness of this feast, took place in two nations, during two different time periods, but each had a tremendous impact on us today. The kingdoms of Egypt and Israel, and even Rome, were rocked to their core and were never the same after their encounter with the King of the Passover.

The Pharaoh of the first Passover, as previously mentioned, was not only a bad student of history, he was also a foolish leader. He became a victim of his own pride and arrogance. Although he was surrounded by the "wise men" of his kingdom, he never seemed interested in the wisdom of the King of the universe. And when he persisted in his hardhearted response to Moses and Aaron (the King's ambassadors), there was a clash of kingdoms. This reaped a devastating harvest for Pharaoh.

In ancient times, it was believed that the largest, most prosperous, and powerful nations of their day was a result of that nations' worship of the most powerful god. They believed that the worship of the nation was to be judged by the power and influence of the society. Good call, as long as you had *all* the information you needed to make a wise decision!

Egypt became the most powerful and prosperous nation of its day, therefore, the world must have believed they had the proper system of worship. There was also a prevailing belief that gods were territorial, as well as regional. They were believed to hold influence over various peoples and nations. I am certain, Pharaoh never even considered that the main reason Egypt was so blessed as a nation was directly linked to the growing number of Abraham's descendants living as slaves amongst them.

Each time Pharaoh rejected the demands of the God of the Hebrews, there were consequences for his stubbornness. His initial response to Moses' demand to set the people free was that he had never heard of this God of the Hebrews. And why should he listen to a God who wasn't even powerful enough to free His own people? Well, things were about to quickly change!

Each time the call was made to "Let My people go so they might worship Me," Pharaoh stiffened his neck a little more and rejected the command. What followed was a series of plagues and devastation, which struck the land hard—the produce, flocks, and eventually, the people themselves.

Have you ever stopped to consider what the plagues were, or why the King chose that exact form of judgment? The answer to that question can be seen in Scripture. This was a war of kingdoms, and the King of the universe wanted to display His splendor and glory for all the peoples of the earth to see. So how do you show the world that the God of the slaves is mightier than all the gods of Egypt? By calling out their gods, one by one, and demonstrating they had no power whatsoever.

Just as a side note, I am compelled to tell you something about our King that may not be readily apparent on the surface—His heart motivation. He is not some egomaniac looking for a good excuse to destroy what He made. He is not a seven-year-old, who is building sand castles at the beach only to stomp them into the ground at the least little whim or provocation. Rather, I believe the heart of God in all His work, and even in His judgment, is the salvation and deliverance of *all* His creation. You see a picture of this even in the Passover Seder (the traditional meal at Passover that tells the story of the deliverance of Israel from their bondage as slaves in Egypt. It is this meal that Jesus celebrated with His disciples, which has come to be known as "The Last Supper" and the third cup and afikomen bread, which is called "communion") when our cup of joy is diminished by ten drops when the plagues are recited. You can also hear His heart for the salvation of the invaders of Israel in Psalm 83, and many other places, as well. His name is Savior, Deliverer, Redeemer, and El Gibor, Mighty God!

The Egyptians worshiped the Nile River as the giver of life. Every springtime, this mighty river, which teemed with fish and life-giving water, overflowed its banks. It watered the dry, thirsty ground so it could produce the abundant crops necessary to feed the people. Rather than worshiping and thanking the King who made the river and ordered its course, the people worshiped the river itself, as the source and giver of all life. So the God of the Hebrew slaves turned the entire river, and all the water sources of the land, into blood. The river, which once brought life and refreshment, now only produced the rancid stench of death. Not only was it no good for drinking, but it couldn't be used for crops or herds of animals. Everything in the river died, as did everything living near the river. So much for the god of the Nile…next!

The Egyptians worshiped frogs as having the power of fertility. The King said, "So you like frogs, do you? Here you go! Have so many frogs that you won't want to see another one as long as you live!" There are songs that children still sing today at Passover that make fun of

Pharaoh's plight of frogs in his bed, in his food, and his cooking pots.

Egyptians worshiped the sun as god (called Rah), so the King blotted it out of the sky. The darkness was so thick that a man couldn't even see his own hand in front of his face.

One by one, the God of the slaves devastated the worship of the Egyptians until there was only one god left standing. The people worshiped Pharaoh and his son, as gods descended directly from Rah himself. You might think that after the King took out Rah, Pharaoh's next of kin, Pharaoh would have chosen his next move a little more carefully. But no, he climbed right back into the ring, with his gloves on, ready for the tenth and final round. This time, Pharaoh's stiff neck not only cost him a son, but every Egyptian home cried out that night because of the loss of their firstborn.

The battle was nearly finished, except that the mightiest army in the world was still intact. But you know how they came to their end. After the death of all the firstborn in Egypt, Pharaoh changed his mind and told the Hebrews to leave his country. As they fled that place in haste, they came to a great body of water called the Red Sea. While the Israelites planned how they might get around this huge blockade, they were suddenly shocked to see the entire Egyptian army coming after them with death in their eyes. Trapped between water and mountains, the Israelites cried out to the God, who had delivered them from slavery. He heard their cry. Following God's directive, Moses stretched his staff out over the waters and the waters parted. The Bible says God blew on the water, creating a wall of water on both sides of a dry highway, in order for the Israelites to pass through. Pharaoh's chariots pursued with all their might, set on killing the fleeing slaves. Once the last Hebrew foot had crossed over, the two great walls of water came crashing down, throwing Pharaoh's entire army to the bottom of the sea like stones, drowning them in full sight of all Israel.

What an incredible display of power, faithfulness, and might! The entire nation of Israel had been preserved and protected from those who would destroy it—by the mighty power of the King. This was truly a miraculous event. There was nothing to compare it to in the entire history of mankind. Who wouldn't want to remember this incredible display of power and celebrate the King's victory each year?

Well, unfortunately, most of the Kingdom today is made up of those who are not direct descendants of those slaves and, therefore, feel no real connection whatsoever to them. The recounting of this world-shaking event, and its consequences, is left to the storytellers of Hollywood. They dress the actors up in sandals

If there is only one Kingdom with only one King, then we also have only one history (His story) as a people who belong to His Kingdom.

and robes, and they speak with a British accent (which makes it feel more authentic). We watch the movie screen and marvel at the grace and power of God, but we don't personally connect to the people who were saved, or the King who saved them. What a tragedy! If we are truly Abraham's seed, then they were our family, either by blood or adoption. If there is only one Kingdom with only one King, then we also have only one history (*His story*) as a people who belong to His Kingdom.

What has happened to us as a people?

Why don't we see the King's victories—past, present, and future—as one great continuum of His mighty power for those who are being saved? Great question. Now I have an even more probing question to ask. What would possess the citizens of the Kingdom to not only ignore the history of their own King, but to transplant His victories into the celebrations of the very kingdoms He defeated? Where and when did reasonable thinking depart from us to do such a thing? In our own independence, have we lost all reverence? Who in the Kingdom do we think we are?

To whom was permission given to move the greatest event in history (the resurrection of the Messiah) from its historic foundations during the Passover to another calendar? How did we move away from the Lord's Feast of First Fruits to embrace Easter eggs and chocolate bunnies? Jesus was raised from the dead on the Feast of First Fruits! Many Christians today might say, "Passover...what's that to me? Those sure are strange customs and traditions of the Jews, who were rescued from slavery in Egypt so many years ago. Besides, we have our own celebrations that kind of cover all that, don't we?" Just as a reminder, it was not the Jewish people who placed the timing of the unveiling of the New Covenant during the Feast of Passover and Unleavened Bread, but rather it was implemented by the Lord of Hosts, and His timing is perfect!

Somewhere along the line, our teachers began to feed us from a different table with the foods that *seemed* right to them. During the time of Constantine, who is revered by many as a savior of the church, many things changed. He forbade the use of anything for worship that smacked of those "Jewish roots." No creeds, hymns, prayers, or articles were to be permitted as a part of Christian liturgy, or practice, in the new Roman state religion. The following paragraph is known as *Constantine's Creed*. It, obviously, marked an official end to any historical, Biblical Jewish practice, even the setting of the date to celebrate the resurrection of the Messiah.

I renounce all customs, rites, legalisms, unleavened breads, and sacrifices of lambs of the Hebrews, and all other feasts of the Hebrews, sacrifices, prayers, aspirations, purifications, sanctifications and propitiations, and fasts, and new moons, and Sabbaths, and superstitions, and hymns and chants, and observations and synagogues, and the food and the drink of the Hebrews. In one word I renounce everything Jewish, every Law, rite and custom; and if afterwards I shall wish to deny and return to Jewish superstition, or shall be found eating with Jews, or feasting with them, or secretly conversing and condemning the Christian religion instead of openly confuting them and condemning their vain faith, then let the trembling of Cain and the leprosy of Gehazi cleave to me, as well as the legal punishments to which

I acknowledge myself liable. And may I be an anathema in the world to come, and may my soul be set down with Satan and the devils...Furthermore: I accept all rights, legalism and feasts of the Romans, sacrifices, prayers, purifications of water, sanctifications by the Pontificus Maximus, propitiations, feasts, and the New Sabbath, Sol Dei (Day of the Sun), all new chants and observances, and all the foods and drinks of the Romans. In other words, I absolutely accept everything Roman, every new law, rite and custom of Rome and the New Roman Religion.

— Emperor Constantine

Here is yet another statement attributed to the Emperor Constantine, which followed the council he convened at Nicaea in the year 325. Although his intent was to bring unity and uniformity to the newly established Roman state religion, you can see why there would be a radical and cataclysmic break with history and Jewish believers in particular.

At the council we also considered the issue of our holiest day, Easter, and it was determined by common consent that everyone, everywhere should celebrate it on one and the same day. For what can be more appropriate, or what more solemn, than that this feast from which we have received the hope of immortality, should be kept by all without variation, using the same order and a clear arrangement? And in the first place, it seemed very unworthy for us to keep this most sacred feast following the custom of the Jews, a people who have soiled their hands in a most terrible outrage, and have thus polluted their souls, and are now deservedly blind. Since we have cast aside their way of calculating the date of the festival, we can ensure that future generations can celebrate this observance at the more accurate time which we have kept from the first day of the passion until the present time…

— Emperor Constantine

There have been many more since the time of the emperor, including even the great reformer Martin Luther, who spoke against such practices and traditions of the Jews with varying degrees of viciousness and passion. Some would later be recognized as blatant anti-Semitic, while others simply thought it best not to continue in the ways of a nation that dismissed its own Messiah. Some see the practice of Kingdom holidays as re-erecting the wall of partition, which Jesus broke down in His own sacrifice and resurrection. But doesn't it seem odd then that the King, specifically and intentionally, chose to fulfill His Word and display His glory during these very feasts and celebrations?

Just recently, I had the honor and privilege of helping a church in Manhattan celebrate the rebirth of the modern State of Israel. There were banners and music, special guests from the Israeli Embassy, and a Jewish archeologist, who amazed everyone there with some of his firsthand stories of diggings and excavations in the land of Israel.

After the festivities came to a close, George, the archeologist invited some of us to join him for dinner at one of his favorite New York City restaurants. This man is Jewish, but he is not yet a believer in Messiah, nor is he even a religious Jew. In fact, he is over the age of sixty-five, and this was his first experience inside a church! He told us why he had never been in a church before, how he had experienced intense anti-Semitism while growing up in an ethnic neighborhood on the west side of Cleveland—very sad and completely embarrassing to the believers at the table. (As it turned out, I discovered that we had both attended the same synagogue in downtown Cleveland during the late 1960s—*small world!*)

After listening to the conversation of some of the pastors around the dinner table, George seemed a little perplexed. Without warning, he blurted out a question, which was the source of his dilemma. "Why don't Christians celebrate Passover?" he asked. "Don't you believe that Jesus is the Passover Lamb? Wasn't He raised from the dead on the Feast of First Fruits? Isn't He the unleavened bread without sin? Isn't communion an abbreviated Passover Seder?"

"Why don't Christians celebrate Passover?" he asked. "Don't you believe that Jesus is the Passover Lamb? Wasn't He raised from the dead on the Feast of First Fruits? Isn't He the unleavened bread without sin? Isn't communion an abbreviated Passover Seder?"

I was sitting right next to George, as he asked his probing and thoughtful questions. I thought, "Man, I couldn't have said it any better myself!" The table became quiet—as pastors, apostles, and prophets—considered how to answer his hosts of questions. In the few tense moments of silence which followed, I leaned over to George and whispered, "Preach it George, preach it!"

Israel's Messiah

Let me make two more remarks here before moving on. First of all, if Israel had recognized Yeshua the first time and crowned Him as King, He could not have been the long-awaited Messiah. Why? Because the prophet Isaiah, in his detailed description of the Anointed One, beginning in chapter fifty-two, verse twelve, and continuing right on through chapter fifty-three, clearly stated that the true Messiah would be "despised and rejected, not esteemed, led as a lamb to the slaughter, buried with the poor and the rich in death"—certainly not the welcoming reception one would give to royalty! But because these words were fulfilled to the letter, we can clearly see that Yeshua is indeed the one described by the prophet so many years before.

Secondly, Jesus was not rejected by the entire nation, but was received and worshiped as Messiah by a large minority of the people. Some scholars put the number of followers of Yeshua during the first century at somewhere around one million people—nearly one sixth of all Israel! (Dr. Pinchas Lapide, an Orthodox Jewish scholar presents this number in his book: *The Resurrection of Jesus, A Jewish Perspective.*)

It was, in fact, the spiritual leadership, or Sanhedrin, who rejected Him as Messiah and again—not *all* did. Because of His growing popularity, they may have feared an uprising among the people to crown Him King of Israel, possibly inviting a Roman massacre to end the revolt. But even so, not all of the leaders rejected him.

And, how could Yeshua be the *Passover* Lamb, the One who takes away the sin of the world, if He had not first been examined by the high priest, then handed over to the Romans for execution on the Feast of Passover, and later raised from the dead on the Feast of First Fruits (Leviticus 23)? The Holy Spirit was poured out on the Jewish followers of the Jewish Messiah during the Feast of the Lord at Shavuot/Pentecost in Jerusalem. The ancient pattern continues and will continue until the word of Paul in Romans 11 is fulfilled and all Israel is saved.

Let me give you an example here from the life of Joseph that will help you understand why I am so passionate about the Calendar of the Kingdom and the *how*, *when*, and *why* we celebrate. Joseph grew up with his brothers until he was seventeen years of age. He was then sold as a slave, by his brothers, to some Ishmaelites, who were on their way to Egypt. You know the story well of his faithful service as a slave, his imprisonment on false charges, and his eventual rise to an Egyptian throne as the second most powerful man in the world. I bring this story to your attention because of the curious circumstances under which Joseph is finally revealed and reunited with his brothers. When the terrible famine of the day finally reached Canaan, Jacob sent ten of his sons down to Egypt in order to buy grain and save the family from starvation. Here's the curious thing; when the ten sons of Jacob came before Joseph to buy grain…not one of them recognized him! Why? Because he looked like an Egyptian, he dressed like an Egyptian, he smelled and spoke like an Egyptian. He was called by an Egyptian name, and he even spoke to them by way of an interpreter. Joseph was, in fact, a prince among his own people, but because he was so carefully removed and completely absorbed, Joseph was unrecognizable for who he *truly* was.

Do you see where I am going with this? Yeshua is a prince among His people, but because He has been so carefully and methodically removed from His land and culture, He is unrecognizable by His own brothers as the Jewish Messiah. His name has been changed; even His culture and clothing have been changed. When He's depicted in movies, He has a distinct British accent! And for some 1,700 years or more, His great victories and celebrations (the Feasts) have been moved to another calendar and time—or ignored all together! I, for one, am anxious to help Yeshua remove His Egyptian costume so that His brothers (the Hebrews) will recognize and embrace Him, once again, for who He *truly* is—King of the Jews.

Dump Da Bunny / Whack Da Wabbit

So what is it about chocolate Easter bunnies, colored-egg hunts, baskets, parades, and bonnets, which capture the attention, resources, and affection of so many believers? Do we not recognize the traditions of pagan gods with "rites of spring," fertility cycles, or even worse—do we just not care?

When did we trade our Passover Lamb for an Easter ham? What was so wrong with celebrating the greatest victories of the King and His Kingdom, on the days in which they historically and biblically occurred? Wouldn't that be the reasonable way to do things? What is so foreign about Passover, the Lord's Feast of Unleavened Bread, and First Fruits that we feel compelled to embrace these "better" ways to celebrate the gift of the Jewish Messiah?

Have you ever been to Israel or visited a religious Jewish town or neighborhood during a feast or festival? I think you might be surprised or even convicted by their obviously Biblical expressions. For instance, on the Feast of Esther, (not a major holiday) families share a special dinner and the book of Esther is read aloud in its entirety. The children dress up like one of the characters in the story—Esther, Mordecai, Haman, etc. They take part in the story-telling by making hissing noises whenever Haman's name is read, and cheering whenever Mordecai's name is heard. At Passover, the special Seder is enjoyed by the entire family as the story of deliverance from Egypt unfolds during the meal. The days in between Passover and Pentecost (Shavuot) are counted down, day by day, in the Counting of the Omer. Pentecost is celebrated with Torah scrolls and dancing, in thanksgiving to God for providing His covenant Word. Hanukkah is celebrated every day of the feast by lighting the menorah (hanukiah), with singing and playing of games, in remembrance of the victory of the brave Maccabees over the huge Syrian army and the miracle of the oil that burned for eight days.

Christians, on the other hand don't celebrate Passover, we celebrate the resurrection of Messiah on the biblical Feast of…Easter? Yup, Easter. And we do so with bunnies, bonnets, baskets, and Easter egg-hunts. We do all of these things because they remind us of the story of…in the Book of…and it teaches our children about…and it draws us closer to the God we love because…I think you get my drift here. Then we gather the family around the table for a feast of the most unkosher foods that can be provided, maybe saying in effect: No Jews are welcome here! If this sounds harsh, just think about it for a moment. The feast is clearly removed from its biblical place. It is then celebrated with extra biblical elements and foods that are not welcoming to the lost sheep from the house of Israel.

Okay, so we don't do a respectable job of celebrating His death and resurrection, but what about His birth? Well, we sing a Christmas carol or two at church. We then cut down a tree, drag it inside, and decorate it with all kinds of stuff we've collected over the years. Then we buy lots of gifts for each other and place them under the tree, to be opened at the appropriate time. Of course, this action is in order to remind us of what is written in the Book of…hmmmmm.

Why don't these things bother us? Do we give any thought to them, or do we just march in step with whatever we experienced growing up? Year after year, we repeat the same traditions, while we make the same lame excuses about why we do what we do and when we do it. Have we become that dull? Do our teachers and prophets have absolutely nothing to say about these things? Have we become a *religion* that is so completely removed from its roots that we wouldn't recognize a Kingdom celebration if it jumped up and bit us where it hurts?

On a personal note, I can remember so clearly an event which may shed some light on the previous paragraphs. Sometime after I was born-again and married the love of my life, our home was blessed with the birth of our first son, Nathan. By the time he was two years old, my dad expected him to follow in the traditions of our culture and wanted some pictures of what his grandson looked like as we took him out "trick-or- treating." I calmly tried to explain to my father that we would not be dressing our son up as a demon, a monster, Count Dracula or any other personage. Also, we would not be taking him door to door begging for sugar! I might as well have told my dad that we would not be sending him to school or letting him drive a car when he came of age! "What kind of parents are you?" he asked, with a noticeably irritated voice. Are you some religious nut case now that you would deny your son this enjoyment? He went on for a while in this manner, until it became obvious that I was unmoved by his passion to allow our son this simple pleasure of our culture.

Some of us call ourselves "Word of Faith" and then completely ignore the Word of God with respect to the issues I have raised. I will tone down my rhetoric now and simply say that the reasons, and perhaps the best reasons, for this attitude is due to centuries of disconnect and a severe lack of sound teaching about the King and His Kingdom.

So now I ask, where is our sense of humility and gratitude? Where is our passion for the holiness of the One who redeemed our fathers and us, by His own glory and goodness—the One who is faithful to fulfill every word that proceeds from His mouth? It seems to me that our ways could use a sober re-examination.

The Passover Fulfilled

Now back to Passover. So the Exodus, with all the miracles, battles, and movies, is not enough to bring us together at the table. But what do we do with the fact that this was the time chosen by the King to display His most awesome love to the world? It was against this rich and historical backdrop that He offered Himself as the Passover Lamb. He removed the final barrier between Himself and the world, even the sin of mankind. This is the perfect stage for the event itself, a time when *a lamb* was offered for the sins of Israel.

Unleavened bread, or matzo, is eaten exclusively during this time because it contains no yeast, which is the biblical symbol of sin. The first Sunday after the Passover is the Feast of First Fruits. As stated by the apostle Paul in 1 Corinthians 15:20, "But Messiah has indeed been raised from the dead, the *first fruits* of those who have fallen asleep." He is the first fruits of those who have been raised from the dead. What an incredible picture of the Lord's grace and love, displayed for all to see. Why would any reasonable individual want to move these celebrations from their original context to a foreign land with pagan temples? And why in this modern era, with all our understanding and enlightenment, do we continue on this path? I keep asking myself these questions.

I have a dream...that one day a group of highly respected pastors, teachers, and prophets will stand up and say, "Enough! After much prayer and deliberation, it seems good to us and the Holy Spirit that we embrace the celebrations of the Lord's Feasts, as He intended all along, and we will begin this year with Passover." May I live to see the day!

Shavuot / Pentecost: The Outpouring of Word and Spirit

Let's move on to the next great celebration of the Kingdom. The Hebrew word *Shavuot* is the word *weeks* in the English language. The instructions in the manual for Kingdom celebrations (Lev. 23) says that from the time of Passover we are to count off seven Sabbaths, and then celebrate this feast with the Lord (this is in May or June). *Pentékonta* is the Greek word for fifty. It is where we get the name *Pentecost* from, as the feast happens fifty days after Passover.

We are familiar with what occurred in the book of Acts, chapter two, when the promise of God—the Holy Spirit—came to those followers of Yeshua in the upper room, but do we know what they were doing there? Some would say they were obeying the command of the Lord to wait in Jerusalem until He gave them the power they needed to be ambassadors for the Kingdom. Yes, that is true. They were doing that, but why were 120 of them gathered in that upper room?

Let's go back to the Scriptures and see. In Acts 2:1, it says, "When the day of Pentecost [or Shavuot] came, they were all together in one place." The cross-reference there to the word *Pentecost* is found in Leviticus 23:15-16, which gives the details for the Feast of Shavuot. The 120 were there primarily to wait for the promise of the Father, *and* they were gathered together to celebrate the victory of the Kingdom (when the Lord had placed His laws of the Kingdom into the hands of Moses on Mount Sinai).

Yes, the first followers of Jesus of Nazareth were celebrating Shavuot, the day the Law was given to Moses and the citizens of the Kingdom. The King Himself confirmed it with signs and wonders. The one who received it on Mount Sinai was radiant with the glory of the Giver for many, many days thereafter. What happened during that celebration in Acts 2 is further evidence, to me, of the blessing from the King, as they received His gracious invitation to celebrate. I wonder: *Would the blessing have been poured out if the believers were all scattered in their homes "waiting" for a visitation instead of worshiping together?* It's just a thought, but it seems to me that the blessing of the Lord is a result of being obedient to the Word of the Lord. I know a lot of our teachers don't like the "*if you, then I*" declarations of the King, but they are evident throughout the Bible. "If my people...then I will hear" (2 Chron. 7:14). "If you obey me...then I will be your God" (Ex. 19:5). "If you obey my words, then you are truly my disciples" (John 8:31). And they go on and on.

In Acts, chapter 20, the apostle Paul is once again anxious to get to Jerusalem if at all possible. Why? He wanted to be there in order to celebrate the two great victories of the Kingdom, which happened on the same day hundreds of years apart—the giving of the Kingdom's constitution (Law) to Moses, and the pouring out of the promise at

Pentecost (see Jer. 31, Ezek. 36, Joel 2). Paul declares in Romans 8:23: "Not only so, but we ourselves, who have the first fruits of the spirit…" Yeshua is the "First Fruits" from the dead, and we are the "First Fruits of the Spirit!"

The blessing of the King flows down to the subjects of the Kingdom. This is clearly stated in Psalm 133, as the anointing on the head of Aaron flows down on his beard and then his garments. We are the body of the King on earth, and His anointing in First Fruits flows over us, as His ambassadors and blessing dispensers. Jesus prayed for us in John, chapter 17, that we would be one body, even as He and the Father are One. "Sh'ma Yisrael, Adonai Eloheinu, Adonai Echad" or "Hear O Israel, the Lord our God, the Lord is One." For those who are citizens of His Kingdom, the blessings of the King are theirs to enjoy.

CHAPTER 10

Celebrate the Future—
The Fall Feasts

Fall Feasts: To Declare a Future Glory

The spring celebrations reflect the first appearing of Messiah, and the fall celebrations reflect His second appearing. Yeshua will complete God's plan for man through the fulfillment of these feasts. He will first come for His bride, to take her to heaven. Then He will return to the earth to judge and cleanse the people. He will then establish His Kingdom on the earth. In that light, they have not *passed away* as some would suppose. On the contrary, they are waiting to declare a future glory that frames the end of time!

The fall feasts include Rosh HaShanah, Yom Kippur, and Sukkot, or the Feast of Tabernacles. When you read through Leviticus, chapter 23, you may not remember seeing Rosh HaShanah in the text. If you caught this, give yourself a pat on the back for being attentive. According to the Torah, this feast is Yom Teruah, or the day for blowing the trumpet. Why is it now known as Rosh HaShanah, the *head of the year,* when we already have a first month back at Passover, Nissan 1 on the Jewish calendar?

Judaism recognizes several *new years* as part of its yearly celebrations. Nissan 1 (March) is the first month of the Biblical (lunar) calendar and is the new year for the purpose of counting the reign of kings and a Biblical year on the calendar. Elul 1 (August) is the new year for the tithing of animals. Shevat 15 (February) is the new year for trees to determine when first fruits may be eaten. And Tishri 1 (Rosh HaShanah) is the new year for years when Sabbatical and Jubilee years begin. This, I will grant you, may be confusing, but it also points out how far off course our "modern" Greek calendar is from the Hebrew accounting, which has a lunar guide based on the cycles and phases of the universe.

Feast of Trumpets: Rosh HaShanah

Rosh HaShanah will not be found in your Bible in Leviticus 23 as one of the biblical feasts. It literally means "head of the year," and is the Feast of Yom T'ruah, which *is* found in your Bible (Rosh HaShanah is 1 Tishri, sometime in September or early October).The rabbis changed the name of the feast many years ago, perhaps during the Babylonian captivity, as it appears on the calendar about the same time as the Babylonian New Year. It is a day for the sounding of shofars, or trumpets, rest, a sacred assembly and sacrifices made to the Lord by fire. In today's world, Rosh HaShanah announces the beginning of the fall feasts and begins the ten Days of Awe leading up to Yom Kippur, the holiest day of the year. The Days of Awe are characterized by prayer and fasting, repentance and self examination in order to prepare for the day when the High Priest would go before the presence of the Lord in the Holy of Holies. In ancient times when the Temple stood in Jerusalem there was a scarlet red ribbon that was hung outside the Temple. If the sacrifice and prayers of the High Priest were accepted by Adonai, the red cloth would change to white. It is recorded in the Talmud that sometime after the death and resurrection of Yeshua…the chord never changed color again!

So now let's take a look at how this fall sequence of feasts might announce more than is obvious to the casual eye. In 1 Thessalonians 4:13, we read these words: "Brothers, we do not want you to be ignorant..." In verse 16, the writer continues, "For the Lord himself will come down from heaven, with a loud command, with the voice of the archangel, *and with the trumpet call of God*, and the dead in Christ [Messiah] will rise first" (emphasis added).

Could Yom T'ruah (Rosh HaShanah) be the announcing of the return of the Lord? Consider Matthew 24:31, "And He will send His angels with a loud trumpet call, and they will gather His elect from the four winds, from one end of the heavens to the other." And in 1 Corinthians 15:51 we read, "Listen, I tell you a mystery: we will not all sleep, but we will all be changed, in a flash, in the twinkling of an eye, at the last trumpet. For the trumpet will sound, the dead will be raised imperishable, and we will be changed." The last trumpet announcing the Kingdom is found in Revelation 11:15, which says, "The seventh angel sounded his trumpet, and there were loud voices in heaven, which said: 'The kingdom of the world has become the kingdom of our Lord and of his Messiah and he will reign for ever and ever!'"

So can we say with complete clarity and confidence that this is how and when the Lord will return to establish the Kingdom and commence the millennial reign of Messiah? Obviously, no one can say that with complete confidence, as no one knows the day or the hour of His return. However, the pattern laid out in Scripture is quite compelling, and the thematic material of the fall feasts is very intriguing to say the least!

Yom Kippur: Day of Atonement

Next on the calendar of the Kingdom (September – October) is Yom Kippur, or the Day of Atonement, where there is fasting and prayer and a whole day for confession of sin. In Zechariah 12:10, we read these words, "And I will pour out upon the house of David and the inhabitants of Jerusalem a spirit of grace and supplication. They will look on me, the one they have pierced, and they will mourn for him as one mourns for an only child, and grieve bitterly for him as one grieves for a firstborn son." In Chapter 13, verse one, it continues, "On that day a fountain will be opened to the house of David and the inhabitants of Jerusalem, to cleanse them from sin and impurity." This is about preparing our hearts for the second coming of Messiah.

The Feast of Tabernacles: The King is With Us!

The story of the return of Messiah continues in Zechariah, chapter 14, verses 4, 9, and 16: "On that day his feet will stand on the Mount of Olives east of Jerusalem…The Lord will be King over the whole earth. On that day there will be one LORD, and his name the only name… Then the survivors from all the nations that have attacked Jerusalem will go up year after year to worship the King, the LORD Almighty, *and to celebrate the Feast of Tabernacles"* (emphasis added).

The Feast of Tabernacles is the last of the three great "pilgrim feasts" that all the citizens were entreated to attend every year in Jerusalem, no matter where they made their home. It takes place in the September/October time frame. So what were these celebrations all about?

One reason for the feast was to celebrate the provision of God during the last harvest of the year. A portion of that harvest was to be presented before the Lord, with thanksgiving for all He had given during the season. Remember what was cursed when Adam and Eve were driven from the garden all those years before? It was the ground. The people had to work and sweat to coax even a meager existence out of the earth. But not in the Kingdom! The feast was a celebration of plenty and of the King's victory over the curse!

When His laws were obeyed, the ground yielded its fruit and there was more than enough to enjoy. So much so, that every seventh year the fields were to have a Sabbath rest and lay fallow for the entire growing season, which means, of course, that the farmers got the same year off from plowing, seeding, weeding, tilling, de-bugging, watering, and harvesting the fields. It's amazing what happens when the King is in charge, instead of a man-directed system. This also means that the six years of planting and harvesting yielded so much fruit that there was more than enough to put away for the Sabbath year!

Imagine what could happen if all the believers took the opportunity of the feast every year and spent those days simply thanking the Lord for His marvelous and bountiful provision for the year.

As a side note here, did you know that when Mark Twain visited the Middle East, back in the late 1800s, he called the Land of Israel a *God-forsaken dustbowl?* It had been pillaged and raped by many Gentile nations, until returning into Jewish hands in 1948. Today, Israel exports more roses and tulips to Europe than Holland! The prophet Isaiah saw this many years ago. He declared that the desert of Israel would blossom and grow as a rose.

Another, and by far the most important reason for this celebration is the desire of the King to "tabernacle" with His people. The command was given to do three things after the crops were all brought into the storehouses. First, they were to take the first and seventh days for rest and fellowship with the King. Second, they were to build a simple booth (a temporary shelter) and live in it with their family for the entire seven days. Third, they were to bring an offering with thanksgiving to the Lord for His bountiful provision. These were to remind us of the time when the Lord brought the Israelites out of Egypt and guided them through the vast desert. He not only kept them, but He protected them from the sun's burning rays by day, under the shadow of His wings with a cloud. He warmed them at night and comforted them with a pillar of fire, which emanated from His presence. For forty long years, their shoes did not wear out and their clothes did not fall apart. He fed them bread, which came down from heaven each day, bread they did not work for or labor in kitchens to prepare. And when they were thirsty… at His command, water flowed out of a rock until millions had more water than they could possibly drink!

What a Mighty God we serve! "Who will not fear you O LORD, and bring glory to your name? For you alone are holy. All nations will come and worship before you, for your righteous acts have been revealed" (Rev. 15:4). And so the Feast of Tabernacles is the celebration of the victory over the cursed ground and over being fatherless and orphaned. We are family. We have a common history and calling as sons and daughters in the house, in the tabernacle of the King.

Before I leave this great event, I must make one more observation. What is the first thing the King will do after He returns and destroys His enemies? It is recorded for us in the fourteenth chapter in the book of Zechariah. (Hint: It will not be an Easter egg hunt around the Mount of Olives!) The prophet declares that all the nations of the earth will be summoned to Jerusalem to celebrate the Feast of Tabernacles with the King. And if for some foolish reason someone should choose not to attend, he will have no rain on his land. Remember, this is during the great Millennium—the 1,000 year reign of Messiah. If these things are on the Father's heart and are so important to Him, shouldn't they be important to us as well?

Much to Celebrate!

He is our Passover—the Lamb of God—who takes away the sins of the whole world. He is the Lamb for every household—a blameless and spotless Lamb. His blood has been applied to the doorposts and the lintels of our hearts. He was raised again from the dead, according to the promise on the Feast of First Fruits and is, therefore, the First Fruits of those raised from the grave. His Spirit was poured out upon those who gathered to worship and celebrate during the Feast of Shavuot, so that the Law of God would no longer be an external code but rather it would be inscribed on a new heart, making us sons and heirs who obey His Law out of love and not obligation.

With these celebrations come revelation, wisdom and understanding, which have patiently awaited an appointed time—a time such as this!

And He will appear a second time with the sound of the shofar of God—Yom T'ruah; then the earth will weep with Jerusalem as for an only son—Yom Kippur; and we will celebrate the Feast of Tabernacles for the Lord is surely with His people. "And the Spirit and the bride say...come!" (Rev. 22:17)

I don't know how I could say all this more clearly, or how else to provoke you to desire these glorious things for yourself. The Body of Messiah, the Church, has been kept from them far too long. The Church has not been enjoying the fullness of her rightful inheritance. With these celebrations come revelation, wisdom and understanding, which have patiently awaited an appointed time—a time such as this!

These are the days of Elijah! Let's celebrate the feasts of the Lord!

CHAPTER 11

He is a Victorious God of Many Celebrations

Purim: For Such a Time as This

As I stated earlier, there are some lesser-known celebrations of victories of the King, and I will address some of them here. There is a Kingdom celebration that most Christians have never even heard about called Purim. In all fairness, though, this is not one of the "big seven" listed in chapter 23 of the book of Leviticus. It is, however, a tremendous story of faith and humility, with all the suspense and intrigue of a Hollywood thriller.

You may be familiar with the basics of the story, as recorded for us in the book of Esther. But have you ever carefully read the book in its entirety and enjoyed the graphic details with all the drama? There seems to be a tremendous amount of material being written right now by some of my contemporaries, who are fascinated by the story.

One such writer is my friend Tommy Tenney, who has inspired us many times with his incredible book *God Chasers,* and his more recent work entitled *Hadassah: The Girl Who Became Queen Esther*, a novel based on the book of Esther. The novel has been produced as a movie entitled *One Night with the King.*

Another friend of mine, Aaron Fruh, who pastors an Assembly

of God church in Mobile, Alabama, has authored a book entitled *The Decree of Esther*. My wife is leading a neighborhood Bible study with outstanding material from Beth Moore on the book of Esther and the challenges women face. This story is not only a look into the past, but also a prophetic word to the Church for this very hour. I am quite certain there is much more being written and spoken along these same lines that I am unaware of, but Esther should be pleased with all the attention she's getting of late! Is there a reason for all the attention?

Esther is the story of a beautiful young, Jewish orphan named Hadassah (later called Esther), who is adopted by her older cousin, Mordecai. In a Cinderella-like scenario, she is selected to be the next queen of the most powerful kingdom of that day. Her storybook life develops a huge wrinkle when her cousin Mordecai becomes the focus of the unprecedented wrath of a man named Haman, who also happens to be the second most powerful man in the kingdom. Next thing you know, Haman asks the king for permission to destroy not only Mordecai, but all the Jews of the kingdom as well. Obviously, there is something much deeper than a personal offense taking place. In fact, it is yet another attempt by Satan to destroy the people God's Kingdom and the covenant promises of the King.

So a dangerous and bold plan is put into motion by Mordecai to save the Jewish people, but he needs the help of his adopted daughter/cousin/Queen Esther. The imagery is so incredible in this story of adoption, then later rise to royalty, and the incredible evil of Haman's plot to annihilate all the Jews. It just begs to be retold here. The parallels between Esther and the Gentile Church, with regard to adoption, favor with the king, and intercession, are simply marvelous. Walt Disney couldn't have come up with a better story if he had tried!

In the end, Mordecai is honored, all the Jews are saved through Esther's heroic deeds, and Haman is hanged on the gallows he had engineered for Mordecai. What a story of strength, honor, humility, and grace! The King worked His intricate plan of salvation, right under the noses of those who plotted the destruction of His people. This is not only a page from history, but like so many things the King does, it has a future prophetic fullness, which is being discovered this very hour.

Purim is a celebration of God's deliverance of the Jews from the hands of Haman, the Agagite, who tried to wipe them out while they lived among the Persians (modern-day Iran). If the Church embraces the King's past victories by celebrating them, I believe she would discover some future glory and callings, waiting to be uncovered. Just ask Tommy Tenney if Purim is worth remembering in the Calendar of the Kingdom.

Let me make one more summary here, if I may, before moving on. Esther was orphaned and then adopted by her close relative, cousin Mordecai. She lived in a foreign land (outside of Israel), she took a Gentile name, she hid her identity, and she was raised to greatness as the bride of the king. But what was the *true* reason she had been placed in the palace? Because THE King was coming—and Israel was being prepared to receive Him.

Now fast forward 2,500 years to today. Again, a Persian (like Haman) has declared he will wipe the Jews off the face of the earth. But there is a queen in the palace! She was orphaned, adopted, grafted in, she lives outside the land, she hid her Jewish roots and identity (really well!), she changed her name, but now she is needed again to save a nation. Her name? The CHURCH! Why is there yet another Persian who is intent on destroying the Jewish people? **BECAUSE THE KING IS COMING!** The Church is needed to take her place and authority, to intercede for a nation and a people; let the Esther generation arise for just such a time as this!

The Year of Jubilee: God Restores

The Lord said to Moses on Mount Sinai, "Speak to the Israelites and say to them: 'When you enter the land I am going to give you, the land itself must observe a sabbath to the Lord'" (Lev. 25:1-2). The text goes on to say that the Israelites were to sow and plant and work the land for six years, but the seventh year was to be a sabbath rest for the land and it was not to be worked. Rest is so important to the Lord that even the fields, flocks, and herds were to be given a regular sabbath rest. So if it is important for the land, how much more important is it for the people?

As we read further in chapter 25 in the book of Leviticus, we find an even more radical idea than resting every seven days, or letting the land rest every seven years. Verse eight states, "Count off seven sabbath of years—seven times seven years—so that seven sabbath years amount to a period of forty nine years." Then the trumpet was to sound on Yom Kippur, marking the beginning of the Year of Jubilee. What was so special about this fiftieth year? All slaves were freed, all lands returned to their original owner, every indentured servant was free to return to his/her own tribe; complete liberty and restoration throughout the entire kingdom!

And what about Jubilee? The simple fact that the King even thought of such a time displays His great grace and mercy toward His subjects. This was a national celebration, which took place every fifty years to rejoice in the King's victory over slavery, lack, poverty, indebtedness, and greed. Again, the Kingdom is not a democracy or a republic, but it is a commonwealth. If one of the citizens had to make the difficult choice to sell himself, or his family or land, in order to pay a debt, it was not meant to be permanent. In the Kingdom, the wealth was to be common to all. So when the Year of Jubilee came, all lands and fortunes were returned to the original owner, to be used for the good of all. No son, or grandson, was held captive to the foolish dealings of the generation which preceded him. Wow! The Jubilee was a victory that extended to every family, in every tribe. What a tremendous blessing to be able to overcome the bad choices your family may have made, which may affect your future prosperity and inheritance.

The following is a brief excerpt used with permission from the book *Israel's Divine Healer*, by Dr. Michael L. Brown.

Closely related to this is Jesus' *jubilee* proclamation in Luke 4:18-19, spiritually speaking, it was time for all slaves to go free and all debts to be canceled. Reading from Isaiah 61:1-2 (with a phrase from 58:6 included), Jesus announced to the expectant congregation: "Today this scripture is fulfilled in your hearing" (Luke 4:21). Then, after escaping from the quickly infuriated crowd, he performed two miracles whose significance should not be missed. These individual miracles are then followed by the healing and deliverance of many and are recorded in all three Synoptics (Luke 4:40-41; Matthew 8:16-17; Mark 1:32-33). Having proclaimed liberty to the captives, Jesus purposefully went about setting them free.

Thus the healing and deliverance ministry of Jesus and his followers was a ministry of restoration and emancipation, to culminate, ultimately, in the glorious liberty of the children of God (Rom 8:19-23) upon the Lord's return (1 Corinthians 15:50-55; 2 Corinthians 5:1-5; Revelations 21:4; Acts 3:19-21). However, our total emancipation was set in motion with Jesus' prophetic, *jubilee* proclamation in Luke 4, and it was purchased and secured by means of his atoning death, by which we are released from the debt of sin.

THE Spirit of the Lord is upon me,
because He anointed me to preach the gospel to the poor.
He has sent me to proclaim release to the captives,
and recovery of sight to the blind,
to set free those who are oppressed,
to proclaim the favorable year of the Lord.
—Luke 4:18-19

CHAPTER 12

The Birthday of Our King

Hanukkah: The Feast of Dedication

Hanukkah, no matter how you spell it, is a wonderful event to enjoy with the entire family. Each year, this Festival of Lights is celebrated around the same time as Christmas. Many believe it is some kind of Jewish substitution for the lights, gifts, and parties of their Christian neighbors. The truth of the matter is actually quite to the contrary.

Nearly two hundred years before the first appearing of Messiah, the Greco-Syrian army under Antiochus Epiphanes invaded Israel with a large occupying force that even included war elephants. When they entered Israel and overpowered the defenders of Jerusalem, Antiochus defiled the temple and slaughtered pigs as burnt offerings on the altar of the Lord. Against all odds, the small Hasmonean priesthood under the leadership of Judah (nicknamed "the Maccabee" which means *the hammer*) stepped up with the obvious intervention of HaShem (Hebrew term for "The Name," an Orthodox substitute for the holy name of God) to defeat the pagan hordes. What an amazing victory that was! Not by power or might, not by overpowering force or strength, but by the Spirit of the Lord!

When the priests finally re-entered the desecrated temple to purify it for worship, they found that only one small vile of holy oil had been spared from the destruction of the Greeks. They placed the small ration of holy oil in the light stand, as they prepared to make the amount of oil necessary for the services in the temple. To everyone's great surprise and amazement, that single day's supply burned for eight days, the time needed to make a new supply.

There are nine branches on a Hanukkah menorah called a *channukiah,* as distinguished from the traditional seven-branch menorah, the symbol of the state of Israel. So if the oil burned for eight days, why are there nine candles? Good question! There is a ninth candle placed in the channukiah called the *servant*, or shamash in Hebrew, from which all the other candles are lit. (By the way, ushers in the synagogue are called by the same name, meaning *servant* or deacon.)

What a great time to celebrate with your family, and give them a history lesson at the same time. It is traditional to celebrate each of the eight evenings with special songs, foods, and gifts. Imagine your home with the entire family sitting around the table, candles burning, and music playing, reading the Bible and imagining how Yeshua celebrated that Hanukkah in John, chapter 10. Pass the latkes (potato pancakes), please!

When is the King's Birthday?

Since every kingdom has a king, then it follows that every king has a birthday. Wouldn't it only be right, then, that the citizens of the Kingdom of God should celebrate the birth of the King of all Kings? So when is the King of Kings' birthday? I know this won't be as popular a subject with some of my messianic friends as the preceding material has been, but here it goes anyway. Setting aside all of the arguments, valid or not, for the secularizing and paganizing of the King's birthday (dare I even mention the word *Christmas*?), let me venture into some holy ground and kick a few holy cows while I'm at it.

We are in trouble right from the start with the date that somebody chose all those years ago. We commonly hear that December 25th is a day chosen for the celebration of many "deities" throughout the millennia. The Druids came along with trees strewn with lights; the Brits love Yule logs, hogs' heads on platters and mistletoe hanging in doorways; Americans embrace jolly old elves, flying reindeer, snowmen that dance, and credit card balances that hurt every month for the entire year. I know all about it.

We all "know" and understand that the reasons for choosing the date of December 25th may not be of the highest intellect—or was it? We do know many things for certain because they are recorded for us in Scripture. Jesus was born to a young, Jewish virgin in Bethlehem (Bet Lechem, or *house of bread* in Hebrew), so He has a birth date. This was a Roman tax season, and there were shepherds tending their flocks at night. There was a most unusual occurrence in the heavens, which caught the attention of watchful astronomers. I have believed, for some time, the best teaching heard to-date, places the time of His birth during the Feast of Tabernacles, making the end of December a good time for the visitation of the angel to announce His appearing (also a good reason to celebrate).

Many factors contribute to this thought in timeline. Perhaps you've given consideration to some of these. Why were all the inns occupied in all of Bethlehem and the surrounding Jerusalem area? Yes, there was a census being taken at the time, but why *then*? Because all the families of Israel would be in Jerusalem to obey the Word of the Lord, to appear before Him during the last of the three "pilgrim feasts."

Consider as well, because there were no rooms available, the innkeeper allowed the young, expecting couple to use his own sukkah, or booth, behind his inn for their immediate need. The word for *manger* in Luke, chapter two, could also be the word for a *feeding trough,* but does not necessarily indicate that the birth took place in a barn—just some more *food for thought.*

Thanks again to my friend and scholar, Dr. Michael Brown, I have been introduced to some very good teaching from Professor William Tighe, a church history specialist at Pennsylvania's Muhlenberg College who states,

The pagan festival of the "Birth of the Unconquered Sun," instituted by the Roman Emperor Aurelian on 25 December 274, was almost certainly an attempt to create a pagan alternative to a date that was already of some significance to Roman Christians. Thus the "pagan origins of Christmas" is a myth without historical substance.

And, just to add a little more fuel to the Yule log, in the definitive *Handbook of Biblical Chronology* by Professor Jack Finegan, the author cites an important reference in a "chronicle" written by Hippolytus of Rome, thirty some years before Aurelian hatched his festival honoring the sun god. Here the Roman historian confirms that these Roman Christians believed that December 25th was the actual birth date of Yeshua.

I believe, we will all agree, that the Lord of the Kingdom does not do anything randomly, or without a purpose. It makes great sense in the natural, as well as the prophetic, that the King would be born during the time when the whole nation was celebrating the presence of the King—during the Feast of Tabernacles. The Lord is among His people. He will *tabernacle* with us. It just makes good sense. But obviously, as I've just demonstrated, no one knows His birth date for certain, as we are not given a date in Scripture.

So, without trying to be too dogmatic or critical, wouldn't it be fair to say that even the King of Kings deserves a decent birthday party? I am even willing to forego the traditional birthday hats and noisemakers, as long as we remember that the promise of His birth and our redemption was, and is, fulfilled in Jesus of Nazareth. After all, which would you prefer…that we bring you cake and gifts on the wrong date or that we completely ignore the fact that you were even born?

CHAPTER 13

Enter into Rest

Sabbath: Come Away My Beloved

I have purposely saved the first celebration listed in Leviticus, chapter 23 for last. I am not the kind of person who likes, or seeks, to be controversial. Nor do I like argument, simply for argument's sake. I never joined a debate team or pulled a sleeping dog's ear just for the sport of it all. But I really desire to find some solid answers to some of my probing questions.

Before moving on to some of these probing questions, let me relay to you a humorous incident directly related to our subject matter here. Some time ago, my dear friend and mentor, Pastor Jack Hayford, founding pastor of The Church On The Way in Van Nuys, California, opened his Bible school for a week of study to messianic pastors and rabbis. All week long we worshiped, studied, read, and listened, as Pastor Jack taught us with sage-like wisdom and deep insight.

On the last day of classes, we were having a light-hearted moment of class conversation before closing a wonderful week. Pastor Jack looked around the room with deep satisfaction and said, "Well, what a fine week this has been. Does anyone have a final question for me?" Immediately, I raised my hand with a burning desire to be recognized, and Pastor Jack called on me. "Pastor Jack, what do you say about the Sabbath?" You might have thought I had just suggested we all retire to a barbecue restaurant for some pulled pork sandwiches! All eyes were fixed on Pastor Jack, as they eagerly awaited his response. He simply stared at me, placed his head in both hands and pretended to weep! "I can't believe it!" he said, "I was hoping to escape this one question, which I did all week, and you have to bring it up at the final bell?!" *Inquiring minds want to know!* He did admit that the subject was problematic for him, especially with the present company, and that was the end of the class.

The words of instruction in Leviticus are so obvious, it would take a completely religious mind (not a compliment, by the way) to mess it up. But it seems to me, over the centuries, we have managed to do just that. The Bible states, "There are six days when you may work, but the seventh day is a Sabbath of rest, a day of sacred assembly. You are not to do any work; wherever you live, it is a Sabbath to the LORD" (Lev. 23:3).

And again Scripture instructs us to "Observe the Sabbath day by keeping it holy, as the Lord your God has commanded you" (Deut. 5:12). I just noticed something else while I was writing this verse from Deuteronomy. All the other commandments, except for one, were stated in a single verse or sentence. This one needed four verses to be declared and carefully explained. Why is that? Why do we so easily dismiss these verses today without so much as a "Father, may I?"

I understand that the resurrection took place on a Sunday, the first day of the week. As I stated earlier, *it was supposed to,* as the Feast of First Fruits, occurs on the first day of the week, after the Passover of the Lord. It had to be a Sunday because Sunday was always the first workday after the Sabbath. (And, yes, I do understand that traditional Jews would date this differently.) But how does that negate, overshadow, make irrelevant, or otherwise cancel the Word spoken thousands of years before concerning the Sabbath?

Almost everyone I have spoken with on this subject, Jewish or not, will agree that there exists at least a *Sabbath principle* of rest and renewal. In fact, I have recently read several great chapters on this subject from Pastor Kerry Weems of Celebration Church in Jacksonville,

Florida. She makes her point from a position of the *rhythms of life,* which are expressed in the Scriptures regarding the Sabbath and the feasts. Her intent is to help us see God's desire for us to be renewed and refreshed. And by the way, I have been added to the staff at Celebration Church to lead a Sabbath service once a month, which we call First Friday. People are coming

If it was important to God, lived out by Jesus Himself, as well as all of His disciples and the first century believers (without question), why wouldn't we see any relevance or importance for our own lives today?

from many miles away, some flying from other countries—that's right—other countries, in order to participate in these services!

Some people, of course, will argue that I am being a legalist, or even worse—a modern day Judaizer, just for bringing up the subject. On the contrary, I am simply saying that if it was important to God, lived out by Jesus Himself, as well as all of His disciples and the first century believers (without question), why wouldn't we see any relevance or importance for our own lives today? What about Paul's warning to the Colossians, you may ask? Well, let's look at it here:

> *Therefore do not let anyone judge you by what you eat or drink, or with regard to a religious festival, a New Moon celebration or a Sabbath day. These are a shadow of the things that were to come; the reality, however, is found in Christ.*
>
> —Colossians 2:16-18

First of all, I am not judging anyone or anything. As I stated at the outset of this work, I am simply asking a lot of questions. And second, if this Calendar of the King, and His appointed times, were already fulfilled (as in passed away) in Christ, then why on earth will we celebrate them again upon His return, when He sets up the Millennial Kingdom and sits on the throne of David in Jerusalem? If we have the complete reality of all things right in front of us, why bother making all the nations come to Jerusalem to celebrate the Feast of Tabernacles? Maybe, just maybe, we are missing something in so readily dismissing these appointments. My question still remains— *why are these celebrations so seemingly important to God, and so seemingly unimportant to us?*

So what is the great victory of the Sabbath? It is the victory of resting in faith that the King who told us to rest will meet all our needs according to His riches and not according to the sweat of our brow. It is a victory over the flesh and a spirit of greed or anxiety. In Psalm 127:2 it states, "In vain you rise early and stay up late, toiling for food to eat—for he grants sleep to those he loves." An alternate rendering of this verse (notated in the footnotes of my NIV) says, "In vain you rise early and stay up late ...for while they sleep he provides for those he loves!" What an amazing God we serve!

Wouldn't you agree with me that there is a blessing for walking in faith and trust in the Lord? What happened to the manna when the Israelites got greedy and tried to gather enough for several days instead of their daily provision? It was wasted labor for them because it rotted

When we are obedient, we will eat the good of the land and find rest for our souls along the way.

overnight. But why didn't the manna rot in the jars when they gathered enough to carry them through the Sabbath? I believe it was because the Lord was teaching all of us about provision...obedience is always better than a sacrifice, and every good thing comes from the Lord. When we are obedient, we will eat the good of the land and find rest for our souls along the way.

When you feel pressured and pressed to make your business grow, or to feed your family, it takes faith to rest. It takes faith to sow your tithes and your offerings, to slow down and take time for family and the house of the Lord. But this faith will produce great victories in our lives if we will only trust in the Lord and in His Word. Let's read about the blessings described in Scripture for those who trust the

Lord and rest as He commanded:

> *If you keep your feet from breaking the Sabbath*
> *and from doing as you please on MY holy day,*
> *If you call the Sabbath a delight and the LORD's holy day*
> *honorable,*
> *and if you honor it by not going your own way*
> *and not doing as you please or speaking idle words,*
> *then you will find your joy in the Lord,*
> *and I will cause you to ride on the heights of the land*
> *and to feast on the inheritance of your father Jacob.*
> *The mouth of the Lord has spoken.*
> —Isaiah 58:13-14 (emphasis added)

How can we jump and shout about the promise in Deuteronomy 8:18 (as a covenant promise of economic blessing), and then completely disregard what He said to do only a few pages earlier in chapter five? Some would argue that the Torah is only incumbent upon the Jews. Well then, stop trying to rob the blessing of the Jews by claiming the promise of the Torah in Deuteronomy chapter eight, while at the same time disregarding *the conditions* for the blessing in chapter five! After all, Deuteronomy comes quite a few books before Matthew. But then again, so does the promise of the New Covenant in Jeremiah 31 and Ezekiel 36, as does the promise of the King's appearance in Psalms and Isaiah. And by the way, who gets to decide what is and isn't pleasing to the King anyway—the priest, the pastor, the bishop, the Pope…you? Why not the butcher, the baker, and the candlestick maker? They all deserve a vote in this thing, don't they?

Isn't there a spiritual fulfillment for all of this? (You know how we love to spiritualize stuff!) For example, in Matthew 11:28-30 when Yeshua says, "Come to me, all you who are weary and burdened, and I will give you rest. Take my yoke upon you…and you will find rest for your souls." Isn't Jesus the Lord of the Sabbath? Yes—without question! But remember what *fulfilled, plero-o* means? Remember, it is not *passed away,* as in *has no significance anymore, sayonara, hasta luego, baby*! Also, remember that Jesus isn't even speaking about the Sabbath here. He deals with that religious spirit in the following chapter.

So do I believe that *all* Gentile Christians are commanded to observe the seventh day Sabbath? In a couple words — Not necessarily. But I would also ask the question: What does it mean to be grafted into the commonwealth of Israel? And this question also takes me back to the query, are we grafted into a religion or a Kingdom? On the other hand, are the Jews under a covenant with the God of Abraham, Isaac and Jacob, and are these Sabbaths and moedim (appointed times) expected to be observed by them as an everlasting sign of this covenant? In a word — yes.

You see, being a Jew is more than who your parents might be, or possessing a certain combination of chromosomes or DNA. Instead, it is a calling and a birthright that also comes with a certain responsibility. The call to Israel, as a priestly nation among the nations, has been (whether fulfilled or not) to know the God of Abraham, Isaac and Jacob, and to make Him known. Being a living witness to the God of Israel and his faithfulness is also a large part of this identity. There is a famous saying in the Jewish community: "I was born a Jew, and I'll die a Jew." The Lord has sworn that as long as there is a sun, moon, and stars, there will be a Jewish nation as a testimony of His faithfulness (Jer. 31:35-36). So the Jewish community is a living and irrefutable witness to the faithfulness of the God of Israel, the Father of our Messiah and King.

One more thought here before moving on. Isn't the call on Israel exactly the same call that was placed upon the Church? To know the God of Abraham, Isaac and Jacob, and then to make Him known to the world? And is there not a clear mandate in Scripture to make Him known "to the Jew first and then also to the Greek [Gentile]?"

Why do we all agree as to the sacred, holy and irrefutable nine commandments and simply discard one as some kind of red-headed stepchild? Why do we get so upset that Alabama Supreme Court Justice

Roy Moore endured so much persecution, and even lost his job, over the battle to keep a Ten Commandments monument in the state judicial building's rotunda (in 2003), when we don't live by these statutes ourselves? Quite honestly, we really don't even like commandments, do we? For many, these are simply the Ten *Suggestions!*

And what is the fruit of our modern enlightened state? The truth is that stroke, heart disease and heart failure due to overwork and stress is skyrocketing in this country. I believe, if we continue to refuse the God ordained cycle of work, worship and rest, we will continue to repeat this awful pattern, enjoying our lives less and less. We are lengthening our years with proper nutrition and medicine, but are we increasing the quality of our days, as well? Is the quality of those extra moments we have purchased really worth it? Or are we finally the product of good medicine and science?

While I'm at it, the divorce rate in the Church is now reported by the Barna Group to be somewhere between thirty-five to forty-two percent, depending on church attendance. We have almost equaled the unbelieving, atheistic world in the destruction of our relationships, and yet we wonder why there aren't as many visitors at the 10:00 a.m. service as there used to be. The seventh (You shall not commit adultery) and tenth (You shall not covet) commandments are quickly following in the steps of the fourth (Remember the Sabbath day), as they are diminishing in matter of importance to believers as we become more like a sub-culture in the nations where we live, rather than being transformers and the counter-culture we were created to be.

Some of our spiritual leaders have even gone so far as to declare marriage to be an *assignment* rather than a covenant. In other words, when they are finished with the current *assigned marriage* they are free to move on to the next *assignment* from heaven. And exactly who gets to determine when the current assignment is complete? Why—the couple does, of course! And following in the same spirit, homosexual marriage is now legal in much of the United States. It is even welcomed in several large church denominations, and while I write these words, the Supreme Court of the United States of America is voting whether to change the very definition of marriage to include…who knows what!

So if we can all agree that the first and greatest commandment, which is to love the Lord our God with all our heart, soul, strength, and might, and our neighbor as ourselves has become too far out of reach, then what we are left with is a much more "manageable" list of our own creation. Praise the Lord! Let's see now, where does that leave us? Only a few more commandments left to negotiate! Good, now we're getting somewhere!

I do hope it is completely obvious that my tongue is hopelessly embedded in my cheek, in order to make a painful point. I would have called these last statements *facetious*, but I simply don't know how to spell that word.

But honestly, why don't we just throw ourselves on the mercy of the court and do what OUR Judge says to do? Why do our denominational handbooks hold such sway over our lives? Why not humbly admit that we are not the King? Why not do what He says, without all the religious excuses and mumble-jumble?

The Kingdom of God is not a mere religion. The Kingdom of God is not about our denominations. The Kingdom of God is not about the traditions of men, which make the Word of God of no effect or importance in our lives. The Kingdom of our God is about obedience and complete dependence on the King. The Sabbath rest, at the very least, should be observed by us all, as we rest in faith in His provision for all aspects of our lives. For the Kingdom of God is righteousness, peace, and joy in the Holy Spirit. By keeping the principle of the Sabbath rest in our lives, we can learn to live with total dependence upon Him. We can trust in Him every day.

CHAPTER 14

Kingdom History and Future

A Call to Embrace the Calendar of the Kingdom

I want to make two points here for observing and embracing the calendar of the Kingdom, even at the risk of being redundant. First, I remember reading as a new believer Paul's admonition to the believers in 1 Corinthians 11, verses 1-2:

"Follow my example, as I follow the example of Christ. I praise you for remembering me in everything and for holding to the traditions just as I passed them on to you."

In verse one, we find Paul encouraging new believers to learn about being a true follower of Messiah by doing what he does (as he learned it from Jesus). The other disciples may have even had a stronger case to say this, as they had walked with Jesus for three and a half years of His ministry. Is it a stretch to say that Jesus kept and honored the calendar of the Kingdom? Why, not at all! We see Him teaching in the synagogues on the Sabbath, in Jerusalem for the Feast of Dedication, Passover and Sukkot, and living a very *normal* Kingdom lifestyle. I would humbly submit to you, then, that Paul learned this growing up, saw it was important to Jesus, and taught it to the followers of God in the nations as good practice, but it was not to be legalistic or binding.

In verse two, Paul declares that he was pleased with them for "holding to the traditions just as [he] passed...on to [them]." The word Paul uses for *traditions* or *ordinances* in the King James version is the Greek word *paradosis,* meaning: *a tradition, doctrine or injunction, delivered or communicated from one to another, whether divine or human.* So as Paul traveled and preached the Kingdom, he was demonstrating, through example, how a believer should live, *and* he was passing on the traditions and ordinances of the Kingdom, as he established local bodies of worship.

As to my second point for observing and embracing the calendar of the Kingdom, I believe it is an invitation to be a unique, distinguishable, and identifiable people on the earth. Listen to these words spoken by God at Sinai to Moses:

> *You yourselves have seen what I did to Egypt, and how I carried you on eagle's wings and brought you to myself. Now if you obey me fully and keep my covenant, then out of all nations you will be my treasured possession. Although the whole earth is mine, you will be for me a kingdom of priests and a holy nation.*
>
> —Exodus 19:4-6

It is interesting to me that in 1 Peter 2:9, Peter changes the words *treasured possession* from Sinai, to *chosen generation* when speaking to the elect who are scattered throughout Pontus, Asia, and more. He tells them that they are not only a privileged people (treasured possession), but they are also a people who carry a tremendous responsibility (chosen generation). Do you see that? They have now been given the charge to carry out the New Covenant with grace and dignity, while separated from their land, people and language—all the things that make a people a nation. Not an easy task or calling.

There are several things necessary to be a nation or a kingdom. There must be a common land, a common language, and a common culture. I submit to you, a large part of a common culture is in their common calendar of national celebrations. Paul tells the Ephesian believers that before following the Jewish Messiah, they were aliens without hope in the world and separated from the commonwealth of Israel—but now in Christ Jesus, those who were far away, have been brought near to enjoy the benefits of the Kingdom. And, Paul continues, even though laws, regulations, and commands were set aside for the sake of the salvation of the nations, there still remains a Kingdom with its people, land, and biblical culture.

Fulfillment of the Feasts

The point of all this is that these feasts, celebrations, and appointed times, are not only a part of our history as a Kingdom, but they are a vision of our future, as well. They are times established by the providence and plan of God Himself. He did this for a purpose, with our own good in mind. He calls us to come aside, rest from our labors, learn from Him, and trust in His unfailing goodness and provision.

> These feasts, celebrations, and appointed times are not only a part of our history as a Kingdom, but they are a vision of our future.

When Messiah appeared the first time, He fulfilled the feasts of the spring—Passover, First Fruits, Unleavened Bread, and Shavuot or Pentecost. When He appears the second time, He will completely fulfill all things, including the feasts.

Listen to the words of Paul in his letter to the Corinthians, as he dealt with a moral sin issue in the Church there.

> *Your boasting is not good. Don't you know that a little yeast [sin] leavens the whole batch of dough? Get rid of the old yeast, so that you may be a new unleavened batch—as you really are. For Christ, our Passover lamb, has been sacrificed. Therefore let us keep the Festival, not with the*

old bread leavened with malice and wickedness, but with
the unleavened bread of sincerity and truth.

— 1 Corinthians 5:6

So was Paul a legalist or a Judaizer, too? Certainly not! He was simply dealing with a sin issue in light of how Yeshua *fulfilled* (raised to its highest expression) the Passover, and He encourages us to celebrate the Feast in the light of this revelation.

A Sobering Word

Bishop Paul D. Zink, a board member and friend of our ministry, as well as the senior pastor and founder of New Life Christian Fellowship in Jacksonville, Florida, had a very interesting encounter several years ago. While on his first tour of Israel, he visited the Great Synagogue in Jerusalem and sat in the visitor's balcony, overlooking the sanctuary. As he prayed, he was suddenly impressed by what he knew to be the voice of the Holy Spirit. The Lord spoke to him very clearly with words that were somewhat shocking for him to hear. *"Jesus would be more at home here than in your church"* is what Pastor Zink heard in the quiet of that moment. What in the world do you do with a word like that? Celebrating the Passover and the Feast of Tabernacles has not won him a lot of *kudos* from the religious community, I'm sorry to say. Being a friend to the messianic Jewish movement, and a lover of Israel, has been the *cause for pause* among some of his peers and contemporaries. But this is a common reaction today among many of our brothers and sisters worldwide, who are unsure, and even suspicious, of the thoughts and intentions of such *visionaries*, or prophets.

A similar phenomenon has occurred with Coach Bill McCartney and Dr. Raleigh Washington. If you recognize those names, there is a good reason. Together they formed and directed the single largest movement among Christian men that the world has ever seen. It is called Promise Keepers and has served the Church to ignite and motivate hundreds of thousands, if not millions, of men across the world to know and serve the Lord Jesus Christ.

But they have received new marching orders as of late. They have come together once again in a new venture they are calling *The Road to Jerusalem,* or *R2J* for short. This is a bold call to the larger family worldwide, to link arms with their messianic brothers to see the Kingdom extend its tent pegs and embrace the modern revival among the Jewish people. This is proving to be more of a challenge for them than they had originally anticipated! Instead of ministering to tens of thousands at a time, the crowds are numbered in the hundreds, and most of them are messianic Jews. I have been on hand to minister and participate at many of these meetings, and I plan to continue this journey with these brave brothers.

Two thousand years ago, the tables were completely turned around. The big question facing the apostles in Acts, chapter 15, was what to do with all the Gentiles who wanted to become obedient to the faith of their fathers and receive the grace poured out through Yeshua of Nazareth and the Holy Spirit. Now we are experiencing the question at a 180-degree turn. What do we do with all these Jewish people coming to faith in Messiah? The first are coming in last, as the Lord prepares to wrap this whole thing up. Before you know it, the nations will be streaming to Jerusalem to celebrate the Feast of Tabernacles with the King of Kings sitting on His throne!

CHAPTER 15

Guess What Time It Is?

Where Do I Get One of These Calendars?

I am very glad you asked! Just remember that because you are switching calendars, moving to a lunar calendar from a Gregorian one, the dates are going to change from year to year. So, the best way to keep up with this is to go to your trusty computer and search the web for a "Jewish Calendar" or "Jewish Holidays" and you will find lots to choose from. Just remember, you will likely be on a religious website that does not share your enthusiasm for Messiah Yeshua...*yet*! (See feast dates on pages 122-126.)

So what does this calendar look like and how do I enjoy it to the fullest? Here's a list of the main opportunities to worship the King and celebrate His victories during the year.

Passover: (March-April) Begins on the fourteenth day of the first month (Aviv) on a Jewish calendar (Ex. 12; Lev. 23; Num. 9, 28; Deut. 16). It's a great time to remember the amazing victory of the God of the Israelites over the false gods of Egypt. Have a family Seder (Passover meal) and pray for the salvation of Israel and your Jewish family and friends. It is also the day of Messiah's suffering and sacrifice for the whole world. The third cup of the Passover (the cup of Redemption) and the Afikomen (the middle piece of matzah separated from the rest) will speak for themselves.

Apr 22, 2016	Mar 27, 2021
Apr 10, 2017	Apr 15, 2022
Mar 30, 2018	Apr 5, 2023
Apr 19, 2019	Apr 22, 2024
Apr 8, 2020	Apr 12, 2025

Unleavened Bread: (March-April) Begins on the fifteenth day of the first month (Aviv) and continues for seven days (Ex. 12; Lev. 23; Num. 28; Deut. 16). This is a seven-day fast from anything containing leaven. For seven days, we remember the leaven of the sin of all mankind that sent Yeshua to the cross, and we remember with grateful hearts our deliverance from bondage, sin and death.

Apr 23-29, 2016	Mar 28-Apr 3, 2021
Apr 11-17, 2017	Apr 16-22, 2022
Mar 31-Apr 6, 2018	Apr 6-14, 2023
Apr 20-26, 2019	Apr 23-29, 2024
Apr 9-15, 2020	Apr 13-19, 2025

First Fruits: (March-April) This begins on the sixteenth day of the first month (Aviv), the day after the Sabbath during Passover and Unleavened Bread (Lev. 23). This is the day of resurrection and new life. A great day to set aside for thanksgiving and praise.

Apr 23-29, 2016	Mar 28-Apr 3, 2021
Apr 11-17, 2017	Apr 16-22, 2022
Mar 31-Apr 6, 2018	Apr 6-14, 2023
Apr 20-26, 2019	Apr 23-29, 2024
Apr 9-15, 2020	Apr 13-19, 2025

Purim: (March) This is the celebration of the victory over Haman the Persian and his planned holocaust against the Jews. It begins on the fourteenth day of the twelfth month (Adar) and lasts for two days of feasting and gift-giving. This feast is particularly popular with the children. Have a special meal and read the book of Esther. (Remember to "boo!" when Haman's name is read!) Special cookies called "hamentaschen" (Haman's ears) are baked and eaten during this festive occasion.

Mar 24, 2016	Feb 26, 2021
Mar 12, 2017	Mar 17, 2022
Mar 1, 2018	Mar 7, 2023
Mar 21, 2019	Mar 24, 2024
Mar 10, 2020	Mar 14, 2025

Weeks/Pentecost: (June) Begins on the sixth day of the third month (Sivan). It is a celebration of the giving of the Torah to Moses on Mount Sinai, and the giving of the Holy Spirit on Mount Zion (Lev. 23; Num. 28; Deut. 16; Joel 2; Acts 2). It so incredible that the Law and the Spirit were given on the same date. This provides deeper insight into God's grace and mercy.

Jun 12-13, 2016	May 17-18, 2021
May 31-Jun 1, 2017	Jun 5-6, 2022
May 20-21, 2018	May 26-27, 2023
Jun 9-10, 2019	Jun 12-13, 2024
May 29-30, 2020	Jun 2-3, 2025

Trumpets/Rosh HaShanah: (September) The trumpet is to sound on the first day of the seventh month (Tishri) (Lev. 23; Num. 29). After the day of the sounding of the shofar, the ten Days of Awe begin. These are ten days of prayerful introspection and preparation for the Day of Atonement.

Rosh HaShanah (Head of the Year) likely came about during the time of Israel's Babylonian captivity, as the New Year in Babylon was around the same time of year. Could this feast reach its greatest fulfillment when Messiah returns with the shout of the Angel of God and the great shofar blast from heaven? (1 Thess. 4:16-18)

Sep 14-15, 2015	Sep 7-8, 2021
Oct 3-4, 2016	Sep 26-27, 2022
Sep 21-22, 2017	Sep 16-17, 2023
Sep 10-11, 2018	Oct 3-4, 2024
Sep 30-Oct 1, 2019	Sep 23-24, 2025
Sep 19-20, 2020	

Atonement/Yom Kippur: (September) This most holy day of prayer and fasting begins on the tenth day of the seventh month (Tishri). (Lev. 16; Lev. 23) Moses interceded for all of Israel, even though he himself was not guilty. This is a solemn day for prayer and fasting for all Israel and for the nations to be saved.

Sep 23, 2015	Sep 16, 2021
Oct 12, 2016	Oct 5, 2022
Sep 30, 2017	Sep 25, 2023
Sep 19, 2018	Oct 12, 2024
Oct 9, 2019	Oct 2, 2025
Sep 28, 2020	

Tabernacles: (September-October) Begins on the fifteenth day of the seventh month (Tishri) and lasts for seven days. (Lev. 23; Num. 28; Deut. 16) Building a booth to be shared by your family can be a deeply moving experience. We eat and sleep in them, if appropriate, to remind us that we are sojourners in this world and that the Lord desires to *tabernacle* with us. As we look up through the branches of our booth and see the stars we are reminded of the promises made to Abraham, and that this world is not our final home. This is also a harvest feast and is celebrated with joy and thanksgiving. It foreshadows the last great ingathering of souls after Messiah comes to rule the earth for 1,000 years.

Sep 28-Oct 4, 2015	Sep 21-27, 2021
Oct 17-23, 2016	Oct 10-16, 2022
Oct 5-11, 2017	Sep 30-Oct 6, 2023
Sep 24-30, 2018	Oct 17-23, 2024
Oct 14-20, 2019	Oct 7-13, 2025
Oct 3-9, 2020	

Feast of Dedication/Chanukah: (December) This happens during the ninth month and is noted on most calendars, whether Jewish or Greek. It lasts for eight days in recognition of the cleansing of the temple in 165 B.C. and the oil supply that lasted for the entire time of preparation. Isn't it ironic that the only biblical reference to this victory of great proportions is in the New Testament Scriptures with Yeshua celebrating in Jerusalem (John 10)? Every night the hanukiah is kindled with prayer, sometimes with small gifts and special foods. It is also a great time to remember Jesus as the Light of the world, represented by the servant candle (shamash) that lights all the other candles each night.

Dec 7-14, 2015	Nov 29-Dec 6, 2021
Dec 25, 2016 - Jan 1, 2017	Dec 19-26, 2022
Dec 13-20, 2017	Dec 8-15, 2023
Dec 3-10, 2018	Dec 25, 2024 - Jan 2, 2025
Dec 23-30, 2019	Dec 14-21, 2025
Dec 11-18, 2020	

Messiah's birth: (December) Traditionally celebrated on December 25th as the birthday of the King. Although there remains great debate about the authenticity of the actual date, it is still the fulfilled promise and a great reason for celebration.

Sabbath: (Weekly) Occurs every seven days and is a day of rest, prayer, assembly, family, refreshing and thanksgiving. (Ex. 20, 31; Lev. 23; Deut. 5)

As you search the Scriptures and read about these events, several things will stand out. One is the number of times the King says, "Do no regular work." These were meant to be times of rest and refreshing, fellowship, and building family and community, as well as worship and giving thanks to the King. Another element is how they are placed throughout the year to give times of refreshment during some of the busiest seasons of life—planting time and harvest time, along with some others thrown in for good measure.

As I write these lines, I am taking the day of Shavuot, or Pentecost, at home with my family. The office is closed, and we are doing no regular work. My wife made a wonderful breakfast for the family of matzo and eggs called *matzah brei*, along with plenty of turkey bacon. Afterwards, I hauled the gang to one of our favorite watering holes— Starbucks—and treated each to his favorite drink. This happens to be on a Monday, before I leave the country on another international adventure, this time to Italy. Yes, there is plenty to do before leaving. And yes, I had to battle my mind about not spending the time preparing to leave with my staff. But I am being blessed for this observance, even as I jot these words to you from my sofa. There is joy in saying *no* to the flesh, to the world, and even our appointment book, but it has to be experienced to be appreciated!

Get-to Do It *Versus* Got-to Do It

So what am I saying, really? Are these invitations from the Holy

Spirit or requirements of the Law? Am I asking the entire Christian community to reverse 1,700 years of tradition and go back to a first-century calendar observation—over night? I offer you a resounding– "NO!" as my short answer. On the other hand, doesn't it seem wrong that we should keep truckin' right along without question, while completely ignoring the celebrations that are so prominent and obvious on the calendar of our King? I believe, there is a much better solution to the *either-or* scenario. That being, the *both-and* solution, which I have alluded to several times in this book. And it may be helpful to know that in some places this attitude has already taken hold with terrific results! Instead of replacing the traditional Sunday morning worship service, some have added a Friday night prayer and praise service. The pastors then teach about these things, while bringing the community together on Shabbat. Perhaps this could replace the mid-week Wednesday service, which so many churches use for the same purpose. When the feasts come up during the year, the church could hold a special convocation and honor the Lord, while teaching about the biblical pattern for rest, work, and worship.

As a matter of fact, we are doing this very thing right here in Jacksonville, Florida. I have joined the staff at Celebration Church as the Artist in Residence, as well as Pastor of Jewish Ministries. My sole responsibility is to oversee a monthly Friday night worship service, which we call "First Friday." We own a Torah scroll that we use on a regular basis. We meet on Shabbat and use some traditional worship elements in Hebrew with translation. Our music and message are consistent with the vision for the services. The attendance last year began at 500 people, per service. Over 2,000 people came to our Passover celebration this past spring, which astounded me! People are driving long distances to attend the services, with some—believe it or not—flying from other countries to enjoy Shabbat first-hand, instead of watching it stream live on their computers. We have a significant number of Jewish people attending regularly, and the gospel is preached with opportunity for salvation at each service!

I would hope by reading this far, you have understood that the

Sabbath, along with these moedim (Hebrew pronounced *mo-e-deem*), *appointed times,* to be invitations and not commandments. These are Kingdom celebrations that extol the King—His life, His victories—and our own history and future as people of the Kingdom. When someone asks the question, "Do I really *have* to do these things?" they have shown that they really don't understand who they are and the depth of what is being said here. They have missed the Father's heart, His plans and purposes for these things. I see in this calendar of the Kingdom a healthy cycle for life—from work, to worship, to rest, and back again, beginning with the weekly Sabbath. Again, we are called, I believe, to live and to propagate a different culture than the one we were born into. Indeed, we are called to live and to propagate the Kingdom culture we were *born-again* into!

In the strictest sense, you could say that God was speaking only to Israel and their physical descendants when He said in Leviticus 23:4, "These are the appointed times of the Lord, holy convocations which you shall proclaim at the times appointed for them." But you can also say that these are a part of *our* history and destiny as the one family of faith called out of every tribe, tongue, people, and nation. In other words, these are not requirements, but they are the *privilege* of citizenship!

In Exodus 33:13, Moses says to the Lord, "...teach me your ways so I may know you." There is an aspect of the nature and glory of God that is only revealed to those who know His ways, who follow after Him with their whole heart and who desire to please Him every day.

Regarding the wisdom in the declaration made by the counsel of apostles in Acts 15, were they actually outlining in great detail the Word of the Lord concerning non-Jewish believers, as they had been grafted into the commonwealth of Israel? Or were they simply setting some basic ground rules for fellowship? Were they speaking at length about how a believer should live, or were they simply asking the Gentile converts to be sensitive and not to offend their Jewish brothers at the dining room table? I believe the answer is obvious and self-evident: The admonishment from the apostolic counsel to the new Gentile believers was for the removing of any obvious stumbling block to fellowship and not necessarily a call to embrace kosher dietary laws. You can probably draw your own conclusion to my position based on what has preceded these few queries, but I will finish the thoughts here for you.

In Acts 15:21, James, (actually his name was Jacob) the brother of Jesus, continues his discussion about Gentile converts and the Law by stating that Moses is preached in every city, in every synagogue, and on every Sabbath. Could he have meant that the new believers would hear and understand what pleases God in the synagogues? Certainly there are accounts of righteous Gentiles who came to believe, and attended synagogue because they had a heart for God (see Acts 13:26; 17:4 and 17). When the new non-Jewish converts were taught the Word of God, they desired to be a peculiar people, a holy nation, a people belonging to God (Ex. 19) in every aspect of their lives, not just doing the bare minimum required in order to get through the door (John 10)!

It is true that the apostle Paul never preached this in any of his letters to the Corinthians, Colossians, Ephesians, or Galatians, but isn't it also true that there simply were no messianic synagogues in the Hellenistic, Gentile world where Paul traveled and taught to recommend to the new converts where they could hear the Word preached and see it lived out in a New Covenant context? There are several other arguments that could be made here, but the question still begs for an answer: *Is the Sabbath still important to God or not?* I get it—*not required*…for righteousness, sanctification, salvation, and holiness. I do understand that, but what did Jesus do? What pleases *Him?* This is still my question, and pleasing God is still my highest pursuit.

Unity for Such a Time as This

So is the Church carnal, apostate, and in need of replacement? Do we place the same judgment at the feet of the Church which has been brought to bear on Israel for generations? Have we now stumbled beyond recovery? Not at all! But we do need each other. If we could all see things with complete clarity and accuracy, then we would have no need for the Holy Spirit. But each of us sees through a glass, dimly. We hear in part, we prophesy in part, we know in part because we are only a *part* of the Kingdom. Jew and Gentile together in the Messiah has always been the plan of the King. It has never been *either-or*, but *both-and*.

There is a word often used these days, which I believe, is very helpful. It is the word—ALIGNMENT. It goes a long way into my reason for writing this book. I believe the underlying questions provoking these pages are these: Are we more concerned about the horizontal alignment with our culture and traditions than we are about the vertical alignment with our Creator and His Kingdom? Have we grown so culturally sensitive and accepting that we are willing to ignore the simple truths about the life and worship of the King of the Kingdom?

Before many of the great victories in Scripture, there came a loud sound intended to startle the enemy. Before the walls of Jericho came crumbling to the ground, there were loud blasts from the shofars. Before the 135,000 Midianites were routed before the tiny band of Gideon, there was the sound of smashing clay pots and shofars. I have believed all these years, that the sound of our shofars and songs of praise like, "Adonai" and "Days of Elijah," would be used by God to bring down walls and chase the enemies of our souls. And, indeed, I have seen these things with my own eyes in more than seventy nations of the world—and counting! But I am not completely satisfied with the results as of this writing. Not enough to put my guitar away and muse about the past victories with friends and family!

Yes, *alignment* is a good word for us today. It may very well be the heart behind King David's words in Psalm 133:1:

"How good and pleasant it is when brothers live together in unity!"

Earlier in this book, we took a look at that word for *unity* in the

Hebrew—*echad*, meaning *one, as in a cluster of grapes*. But I also believe that this word *alignment* is helpful to us now, with a deeper understanding. So maybe we can elaborate, based on the translation of the Hebrew word *echad*, this way:

> How good and pleasant it is when brothers live [their lives in alignment] together [with the plans, purposes and pursuits of their King and Maker!]

I believe I am called to be a shofar (and maybe a smashing clay pot!) to my generation as an advocate for this vertical alignment in song and lifestyle. And so I pray that the God of Abraham, Isaac, and Israel, would give us *all* the humility to hear, the grace to receive, and the courage to obey what the Spirit is saying to the citizens of the Kingdom in this hour. For *Behold, He comes, riding on the clouds, shining like the sun at the trumpet call*. I believe with all my heart, we have *all* been brought to the Kingdom for such a time as this!

I pray that the God of Abraham, Isaac, and Israel, would give us *all* the humility to hear, the grace to receive, and the courage to obey what the Spirit is saying to the citizens of the Kingdom in this hour.

In Closing

King David said, "My times are in your hands" (Ps. 31:15). I believe this is not only referring to the future, but to the *now* as well. In John, chapter five, verse 19, Jesus declares that He only does what He sees His Father do. How much more simple would life be if we could all just live there. *Lord, give us eyes that see and ears that hear!* What I mean by this is simply that in this writing, I want to be cautious that the joy and the freedom I experience through obedience do not become someone else's bondage. Legalism is like an infection that festers and spreads, and eventually, renders parts of the body useless. I want to be careful that my revelation of freedom does not become spiritual bondage to others. When the Lord makes something clear to you, remember that it came by way of revelation and will require the same grace for others to see it, as well.

We will do well to remember what Paul said in Romans 8:14, "For those who are led by the Spirit of God are the children of God." Yeshua sent the Holy Spirit to lead us into all truth, individually and collectively, as Kingdom people. I believe He is doing this and will do it even more, if we will continue to seek Him and His Kingdom first.

Our own personal calendars are marked with special events and celebrations to remind us of the commitments and obligations we have—some that others would agree were important, and some that others may not value the same way we do. It is important to state here that I realize not everyone will see the full value of the things covered in this book, and that's fine with me. As I travel around the world, I am sensing a new awareness and openheartedness to receive and consider some of the positions I have outlined in this work. So as we say in Hebrew...le'at, le'at, meaning, *little by little*.

Thank you for reading and prayerfully considering these things. I believe them to be important to the King and the expanding of His Kingdom authority and influence in Israel, and to all the nations of the earth. May the Lord help us all as we seek first the Kingdom of God and His righteousness!

SHALOM

GLOSSARY

Adonai: Hebrew for LORD, and used often as a substitute for the unspeakable, most holy name of God.

Afikomen: The Hebrew name given to the center piece of matzah during a Seder that is broken and wrapped in a white cloth. It then appears at the end of the meal as the dessert and is purchased back from the children by the leader of the feast. The name signifies, "I will come again" and has a profound meaning for those who understand the life, death and resurrection of Messiah Jesus.

Antinomianism: Is a false doctrine that declares you are saved by faith through grace, therefore, moral law has no authority over the Christian. Made of two Greek words; "anti" meaning against, and "nomos" meaning law.

Echad: Hebrew word for "unity" or "one."

Eshkol echad: Hebrew for "a cluster of grapes."

HaMashiach: Hebrew for "the Messiah."

Hanukkah menorah/Hanukiah: This candelabra of nine branches is used to celebrate the story of Hanukkah and the miracle of the oil that burned for eight days in the Temple.

Hanukkah: The Festival of Lights and also the Feast of Dedication that celebrates Israel's miraculous defeat of the Seleucid Empire of the second century B.C. Although it is not known for certain that a small amount of holy oil burned for a miraculous eight days while more was prepared by the priests, it has given birth to the popular Hanukkah menorah with it's nine branches. The center candle is known as the "shamash" or servant, and is used to ignite all the other candles each night.

Moedim: Hebrew word meaning "appointed times" used of the Feasts and special days of remembrance and celebration.

Passover: The Feast of the Lord celebrating the deliverance of the children of Israel from Egypt and the death and resurrection of Messiah Yeshua. (See Leviticus 23)

Purim: The Hebrew word for "lots" as they were cast by Haman to choose the day for destroying all the Jews of the known world. This is the Hebrew word for the Feast of Esther.

Rosh HaShanah: Hebrew for "Head of the Year." This is also the Feast of Yom Teruah.

Ruach HaKodesh: Hebrew for "The Holy Spirit."

Sabbath: The very first Feast of the Lord that is mentioned in Leviticus 23 which occurs every week at sundown on Friday evening and lasts until sundown on Saturday evening. This is the traditional day of worship for the Jewish community as prescribed by God in the Torah, and was for all first and second century believers. It was probably changed during the reign of Constantine who stripped the Church of any practices, psalms, hymns or traditions that could be traced to the Jewish roots of the faith.

Seder: The traditional Passover meal that tells the story of the escape from Egypt by the Hebrew slaves. The Hebrew word "seder" means "order" as the story is told using traditional food elements in a prescribed order for the meal.

Shabbat shalom: A Hebrew greeting meaning, "peace of the Sabbath," spoken by many congregants at Sabbath services.

Shabbat siddur: This book is a collection of Sabbath prayer and blessings used weekly in the synagogue.

Shamash: Hebrew for a deacon or one who serves in a synagogue. It is also the name of the center candle in a Hannukah menorah.

Shavuot: Hebrew word for "weeks." It is the name given to the festival known as Pentecost as it is celebrated seven weeks after the Passover.

Tanakh: The word for the Hebrew scriptures derived from the three letters T (Torah), N (Neveim, Prophets), K (Ketuvim, writings) This is the entire Old Testament, but the books are given in a different order from the Christian Bible.

Torah: The Torah is the first five books of the Bible written by Moses; Genesis-Deuteronomy. The Torah scroll is a handwritten, or scribed parchment that is given a place of honor in the synagogue and read during the Torah service.

Yahweh: The Holy or unspeakable name of God derived from the four letter tetragramathon, YHVH (yod, hey, vav, hey in Hebrew)

Yehovah: This is another guess at the Holy name of God as is "Yahweh." Biblical Hebrew carries no vowel points and so the reader must know what they are in order to decipher the text. Because this name is never pronounced in the religious Jewish community, there is no real knowledge of the true pronunciation.

Yom Kippur: The holiest day of the Hebrew calendar when the High Priest went behind the veil to make atonement for himself and all Israel. In modern Judaism this is still the holiest day of the year and the synagogues are packed with worshipers for special services.

Yom Teruah: This is the Hebrew name meaning "Day of the blowing of Trumpets." This is also the holiday known as Rosh HaShanah.

RECOMMENDED READING

Brown, Dr. Michael L. *60 Questions Christians Ask About Jewish Beliefs and Practices*. Ada, MI: Chosen Books; Reprint ed., 2011.

Brown, Dr. Michael L. *Our Hands Are Stained with Blood*. Shippensburg, PA: Destiny Image, 1992

Finto, Don. *Your People Shall Be My People*. Ada, MI: Chosen Books, 2001

Intrater, Asher. *Covenant Relationships*. Shippensburg, PA: Destiny Image, 1989

Intrater, Asher. *Who Ate Lunch With Abraham*. Peoria, AZ: Intermedia, 2011

Juster, Dr. Daniel. *Jewish Roots*. Shippensburg, PA: Destiny Image; Revised ed., 2013

Munroe, Dr. Myles. *Rediscovering the Kingdom*. Shippensburg, PA: Destiny Image; Abridged ed., 2006

Teplinsky, Sandra. *Why Still Care About Israel?* Ada, MI: Chosen Books; Revised ed., 2013S

About the Author

As of 2015, Paul Wilbur has been a worshiper for 38 years. At the time of the first printing of *Touching the Heart of God* he has been a traveling musician for over 45 years. After he accepted the Lord Jesus Christ as his Savior, he experienced a radical change. The very next day Paul wrote his first worship song, and he has never turned back to secular music.

Paul Wilbur and his team have partnered with Integrity Music for an astounding 20 years. The journey began with the company's first Messianic project entitled "UP TO ZION," recorded in Chicago, Illinois in 1990. From there, the real legacy continued with the breakout recording, "SHALOM JERUSALEM," captured live in the City of David in 1995. To date, the ministry has recorded four live projects in Israel, two in Texas and one in Florida. With award-winning sales in the millions of pieces and a Latin Dove Award for best live praise and worship album of the year, there is no end in sight for this growing team. Paul has recorded some 20 projects with Integrity in four languages, and the ministry has been seen in over 90 nations worldwide.

In the fall of 1994, Paul was finishing up his fourth year at Midwest Christian Center in Tinley Park, IL, when the Lord spoke to him very clearly and said, "Ask of me and I will give you the nations…" That brief invitation put Paul's life and future on a whole new course. After much prayer, fasting and soul searching, Paul and Luanne announced their departure from local pastoral worship ministry to answer the call of God to the nations. After selling their home, cars, furniture and Baldwin piano, they headed out to do what the Lord had offered them a few short months before. The first phone call of their new lives came from none other than Don Moen of Integrity Music. First, the invitation was to record a new project in the land of Israel. Second, Don wanted to know if Paul was available to do a two-week tour with him in the Philippines. That was the beginning of the ongoing international, cross-cultural, multi-lingual ministry that continues to this day. Two live recordings in Portuguese from Brazil; eight in Spanish, two captured live in Guatemala, Costa Rica, Ecuador and Honduras, and four more recorded live in Israel.

The most dynamic way that Paul and Wilbur Ministries is "changing the way the world worships" is through the medium of concert ministry. When deep streams of worship are married with anointed and timely teaching and preaching, the atmosphere is changed and heaven is present. Prayer and personal ministry are often employed as well to bring the entire room into an encounter with the Living God. An evening of concert ministry with the team is meant to be life-changing and not just a nice experience. Wilbur Ministries truly believes that the Lord inhabits the praises of His people, and in that presence is fullness, and joy.

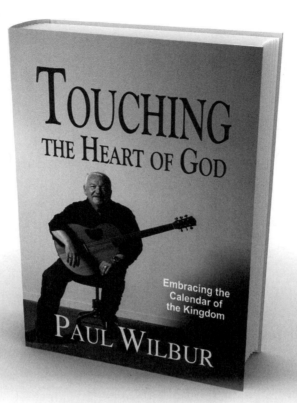

To order more copies of

TOUCHING THE HEART OF GOD,

contact Certa Books

- ❏ Order online at CertaBooks.com/ Touching-the-Heart-of-God

- ❏ Call 877-77-CERTA or

- ❏ Email Info@CertaBooks.com

For additional resources from Paul Wilbur, visit www.WilburMinistries.com

CERTA BOOKS
partner publishing